INFLUENTIAL WOMEN *of* SPOKANE

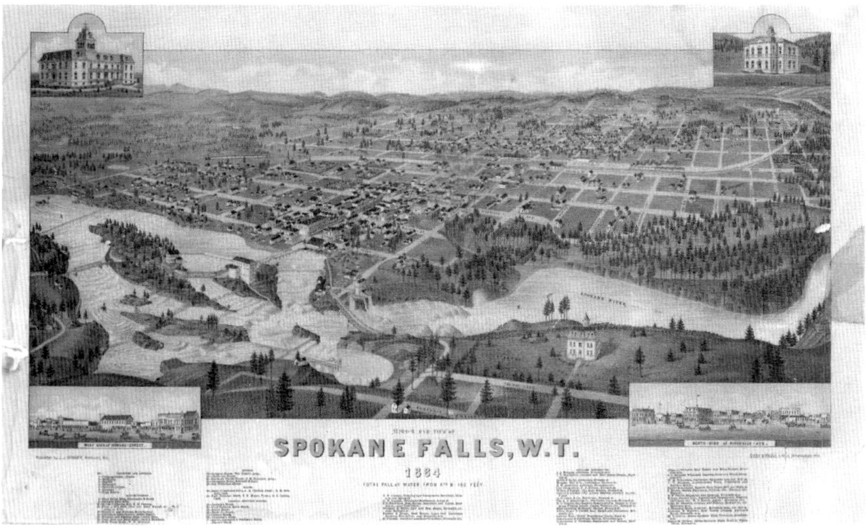

This 1884 map shows the first Catholic church, the Hamblen home and the property Mother Joseph built on. It is the map from which these three details of the property were taken. *Courtesy of the Eastern Washington State Historical Society: Museum of Arts and Culture.*

INFLUENTIAL WOMEN *of* SPOKANE

BUILDING A FAIR CITY

Nancy Driscol Engle

THE History PRESS

Published by The History Press
Charleston, SC
www.historypress.net

Front cover, clockwise from bottom left: May Arkwright Hutton. *Washington State Archives, Eastern Regional Branch, Cheney*; Ella Jones. *Courtesy of the Eastern Washington State Historical Society, Museum of Arts and Culture, Spokane*; Elizabeth Gurley Flynn. *Courtesy of the Lawrence History Center, Lawrence, Massachusetts*; Alice Ide Houghton. *Spokane Falls and Its Exhibition, Matthews Northrup and Co., Buffalo, New York, 1890*; Spokane Streets, corner of Sprague and Post. *Courtesy of Ned M. Barnes Northwest Room, Spokane Public Library, Spokane.*

Back cover: May Arkwright Hutton quotation. *Courtesy of the Eastern Washington State Historical Society, Museum of Arts and Culture, Spokane*; Spokane Map, 1905. *Courtesy of the Library of Congress.*

First published 2017

Manufactured in the United States

ISBN 9781467119863

Library of Congress Control Number: 2017940932

CONTENTS

FOREWORD

INFLUENTIAL WOMEN OF SPOKANE

Visionary and compassionate women profoundly shaped early life in the frontier city of Spokane. Yet they are mostly forgotten. Names like Hutton Settlement, Hamblen Park or Sacred Heart Hospital mark their vibrant contributions, but the paucity of historical records on women leaves us bereft of stories of their lives. What motivated them? How did they demonstrate their concern for the poor, the children, the sick or the women in prison? What public skills, collaborative efforts and strategies did they learn to convince men to give women the right to vote?

Fortunately for Spokane, researcher Nancy Engle brought her formidable skills as a historical detective to write *Influential Women of Spokane*. Sleuthing for years through every conceivable resource to remember and reimagine their efforts, she also offers insight on the community of women who lived in this booming town at the turn of the nineteenth century. Not only does she include fascinating individual stories, such as the two feisty nuns who came to Spokane in 1886 determined to establish a hospital for the needy, but she also invites readers into the culture of women's clubs, benevolent societies and suffragette organizations that gave a measure of public influence. Here women gathered, grew in leadership, experienced failures and successes, but always with a determination to enhance, even "reform" the lives of Spokane residents.

Spokane's contemporary slogan, "Near Nature, Near Perfect," alludes to what also drew men and women settlers to the historic "gem" of Spokane Falls, a turbulent city that grew from three thousand to twenty thousand between 1886 and 1890. Spokane Falls served a northwest region with vast timber resources, rich mining discoveries and fertile agricultural lands in the Palouse. The powerful one-hundred-mile Spokane River and four railroads cut through the downtown. The opportunities that abounded attracted both highly educated families from the East and Midwest who wanted education, culture, newspapers and Catholic and Protestant religious values and also a drifting population of men working in forests, mines and farms who found Spokane Falls as their entertainment outlet. By 1886, thirteen churches, six newspapers, six music societies and railroads coexisted with a thriving raw "open" city serving transient men with saloons, brothels, gambling establishments, Chinese opium dens and shanties. It is in this context that Engle studies the emerging influence of women in meeting the needs of a growing population.

I first became aware of Nancy's intense interest in the history of women when she moved from Florida and was researching the Spokane suffragists for her doctorate at the University of Florida. Around the same time, I was researching the life of Helga Estby, a Spokane mother who walked 3,500 miles with her daughter from here to New York City on a $10,000 wager to save their family farm, a remarkable story that had been silenced for almost one hundred years. Later, Helga became involved in our city's suffragist movement, the area of Nancy's research, and she generously shared all that she had gathered.

Our shared research fields immersed us in the historical reality of how few resources have been kept on ordinary women who lived extraordinary lives in the late 1800s. Engle demonstrates all the essential qualities needed for historians of lost women's lives. She brings creative delving into limited archival resources and a holistic approach in combining oral histories, photographic and social resources. From these pieces she creates a lively and informative narrative of the women who shaped Spokane.

On our doctoral committees, we both benefited from the guidance of Susan Armitage, a historian then at Washington State University who edited *The Women's West*, which grew out of the New Western History conference in Wyoming. They called for scholars to research and write "stories of ordinary women who lived extraordinary lives." Engle's book clearly does this.

In the depth of her portraits of Washington women engaged in the suffrage effort, she addresses the complexities of collaboration that emerged between women over divisions of class, education, religious differences, even "proper" dress and language, often personified in May Arkwright Hutton's flamboyant style. Clear tensions between western Washington and eastern Washington women led to times of explosive conflicts, humiliations, legislative maneuvering and arguments over strategies. Yet they rose above these struggles and never deterred from the ultimate vision of women receiving the right to vote in 1910.

Our city today is renowned in eastern Washington State for the quality and scope of medical care and hospitals; the commitment to education shown through state, parochial, Protestant and city colleges; and resources for children in need. As Engle shows, it's no accident. Yet, Spokane still struggles with how to best create opportunities and services for citizens. With over 16 percent living in poverty, too many citizens still face inadequate health and education programs, and adversarial conflicts continue over the city, county and state's limited resources.

Engle has provided us with our historical legacy, showing that the origin of boldness, vision, passion, practical efforts and determination of strong women became the backbone of today's city. Their spirit of collaboration, acute awareness of needs, willingness to work together on common goals, staying motivated after failure and caring for the common good has the potential to inspire us. This concise collection of *Influential Women of Spokane* offers an encouraging gift for citizens of today.

—Linda Lawrence Hunt
Author, *Bold Spirit: Helga Estby's Forgotten Walk across Victorian America*

ACKNOWLEDGEMENTS

Influential Women of Spokane is based on more than a decade of research. It began in late 1999 when I moved to Spokane. I am indebted to a large number of archivists, librarians and historians. Through the years, their professional expertise has helped me get acquainted with my adopted hometown. My professional and personal gratitude go to Shirley Leckie and Sue Armitage, whose mentorship through the years, has been invaluable. I'm also grateful to Linda Hunt, whose inspiration, encouragement and collaboration means a lot. My own influential women include my grandmother Flossie Morton and mother, Marjorie Driscol. My family, Daniel, Amber and Zach, have been my best supporters as well as my best distractions. I thank you all.

Finally, I hope that while you read this, you will have at least a small portion of the fun that I have had while getting acquainted with Spokane's influential women.

INTRODUCTION

Spokane—pronounced with a short a—is the largest city in eastern Washington. It is most commonly believed to have been named for the region's original occupants, who used a similar word to describe themselves as the children of the sun.

The Spokane Indians, still present in the city in the 1880s, were regarded as silent residents by many white settlers. But they lived in teepees nearby and made their living by selling fish and other trinkets to the white women there. Mary Todd, who migrated to the city in 1894, was surprised when she arrived to find native men and women, wrapped in blankets, walking the streets of Spokane. Likewise, children of the white settlers who built the city of Spokane Falls remembered native men selling things to their mothers, and sometimes, they even played with native children. The earliest school in the region, taught by the missionary Henry Cowley, taught both native and white children. And Father Joseph's earliest plans for Gonzaga targeted natives.

The city was first named for its most remarkable geographic feature, the Spokane Falls. Named by residents excited about the possibility of using the falls to produce electricity, it kept that name until after the fire of 1889. Then city boosters decided that their city would sound more modern without the "Falls" in its name. As growth became the most important aim of the city leaders, the falls seemed more like a tool to help them reach their goals, its beauty secondary. Indeed, population growth would come to the city so quickly during its next two decades that for more than half a century,

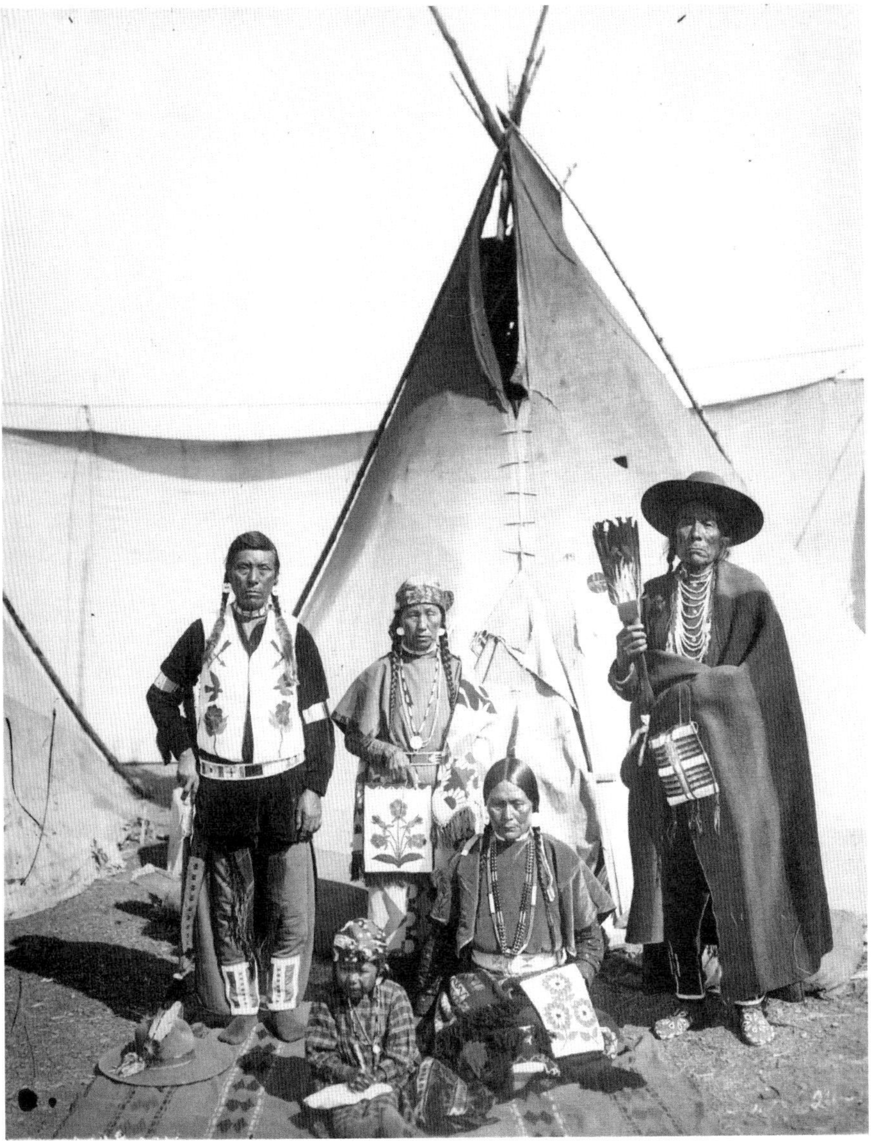

Spokane Indians displaying their wares for sale. *Courtesy of the Ned M. Barnes Room, Spokane Public Library.*

the river and the falls would be mostly covered with bridges for cars and railroads, including a large train station dominating the riverbank. At the same time, mining tailings dumped into the river in Idaho polluted the water with lead. The lead would prove much harder to clean up in later years, but by the late twentieth century, the river would again look like the city's most remarkable geographic feature.

Influential Women of Spokane is set in the city's boom years. Between 1881 and 1910, Spokane grew from 350 inhabitants to 104,402. This large influx of people changed the cityscape rapidly. This trend was especially noticeable in the year following the 1889 fire. City boosters spent large sums of money to rebuild after the fire, and new construction dominated the landscape for the coming year, often designed by architect Kirkland Cutter.

Women featured in this book walked on unpaved streets that turned into ankle-deep mud during rainy periods. They also encountered poor people, many of whom arrived in the city without the resources to pay for lodging, food and clothing. As time wore on, the women who were most economically stable moved away from the city center.

To write more smoothly, I have chosen to drop the "Falls" from its name throughout. I begin with the arrival of the Sisters of Providence in 1886 and end in 1910, after women earned the right to vote in Washington. The two signposts, although important events for women, do not lend themselves to a logical sequence of events. Thus, I have divided *Influential Women of Spokane* into two parts. The first, "Building a Fair City," follows the women who created important city services. It ends in the late 1890s when the institutions were stabilized. The second section, "Seeking Women's Rights," begins with early temperance women who asked for police matrons for local jails and campaigned for the right to vote.

Part One
BUILDING A FAIR CITY

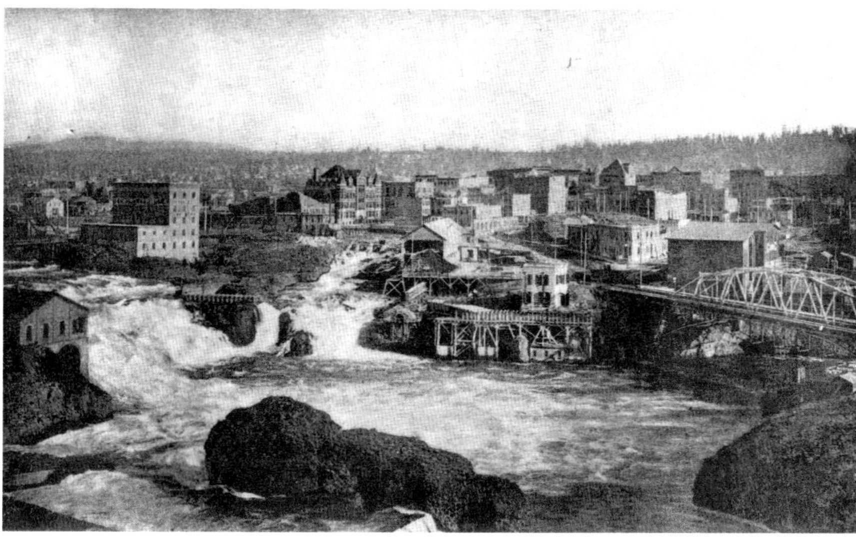

Spokane Falls, circa 1889. Its potential water power drew white settlers to the region. *Courtesy of the Ned M. Barnes Northwest Room, Spokane Public Library.*

1

FROM TOWN TO CITY

In May 1886, Mother Joseph of the Sisters of Providence arrived in the growing town of Spokane, Washington. Excited to be there but tired from the trip, Mother Joseph and her companion, Sister Joseph of Arimathea, might have taken a nineteen-hour trip from the order's headquarters by stagecoach and trains. The need to conserve money, however, led them to forgo the expense of a train ticket and travel overland approximately four hundred miles by canoe, stage and horseback and on foot.

This petite, gray-eyed woman had already completed a much longer journey from her family home in Quebec. Born Esther Pariseau in 1823, the third of twelve children, she was thirty-three years old when she led a team of nuns south along the East Coast of the United States, crossing through Panama and then taking a ship northbound, following the Pacific coastline to Vancouver, Washington, where the nuns created a regional motherhouse. Thirty years later, by the time Mother Joseph had arrived in Spokane, this determined sixty-three-year-old nun had constructed buildings all over Washington.

Mother Joseph planned to erect a hospital—Spokane's first real hospital—and construct a school in Sprague, Washington. Her health facility would be many times larger than the one then serving the town. It would be a place where the city's physicians could practice, and it would provide beds for their patients. And the school Mother Joseph would construct thirty-seven miles southwest of Spokane would be the first of its kind in Lincoln County.

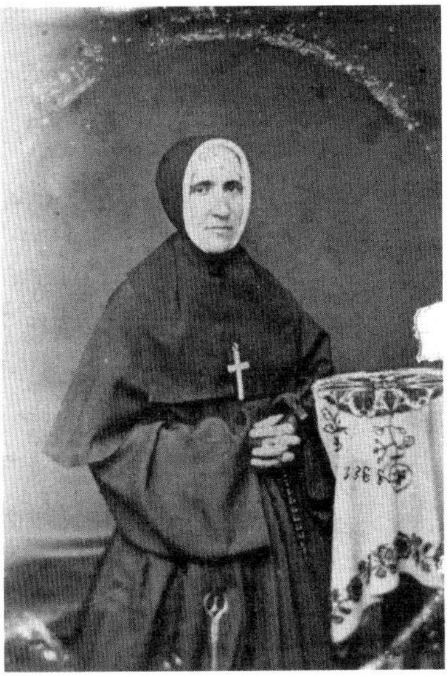

A very young Mother Joseph with scissors hanging from her belt. *Courtesy of Providence Archives.*

In 1886, Spokane stood on the verge of its boom years, having recently topped the population mark of three thousand. Housed mostly in wooden buildings with false fronts, businesses stretched for three blocks along both sides of Howard Street, spilling over onto Riverside Avenue and Main Street. Citizens of Spokane participated in six musical societies and attended thirteen churches. They had a library and a temporary courthouse. For a small town, they had a lot of newspapers—six in all. They could head out of town on any one of four railroad lines. One public school served approximately fifty elementary and high school students, and Spokane College provided further education to a privileged few. One small hospital, the Railroad Hospital, served a limited number of patients.

Father Joseph Cataldo, the region's ranking Jesuit, offered the sisters property upon which to build their hospital, but after inspecting it, the nuns found it unsuitable. The land Father Joseph offered lay across the Spokane River, over a makeshift bridge made up of planks, just north of the end of Howard Street. To reach his property from the train station, for example, one had to take a buggy ride, a boat trip or a long walk.

In selecting property, Mother Joseph followed a Sisters of Providence tradition. In 1843, their founding mother had dedicated the group to minister to the sick and needy in Montreal, Quebec. Émilie Gamelin internalized the desire to help the poor so well that she died of cholera at the age of fifty-one, having contracted the disease while tending a patient.

Mother Joseph's work in Spokane would have made Gamelin proud. She built close to the neediest people. Mother Joseph knew that the poor, who lived near the heart of the city, would have difficulty getting to a hospital situated on the outer limits of town.

So instead of accepting Cataldo's offer of inexpensive land on the north side of the river, she spent $2,300 for property lying on Front Street, only a half mile from the city center. Despite the additional expense, Mother Joseph was happy with the land. "The locality is most beautiful," wrote the order's secretary, "and close to everyone." Its rugged northern edge lined the riverbank, providing a panoramic view of the river just before it divided to go around an island and then over the city's namesake falls.

But creating a hospital in Spokane was challenging. Mother Joseph and her associate lived in a shack and worshiped in a nearby shanty with a simple wooden cross on its roof. Their temporary home was made of rough-hewn planks, with a dirt floor and a leaky roof. Although it afforded them privacy, they had to be careful not to get splinters from the wood. They covered their beds with oiled canvas to protect them from spring rains. These early accommodations in Spokane provided little comfort.

Mother Joseph endured the rough accommodations as part of the sacrifice required to build a hospital for Spokane's sick and poor. Her downtown property proved convenient to the poorest in Spokane, who could walk to the hospital if need be. Her choice of location also gave the nuns themselves better access to city residences, the railroad station and nearby churches.

This central location was an especially good thing for Sister Joseph of Arimathea. She, too, was petite and determined and had made it her mission to help the poor. Her primary job when she first arrived in the city

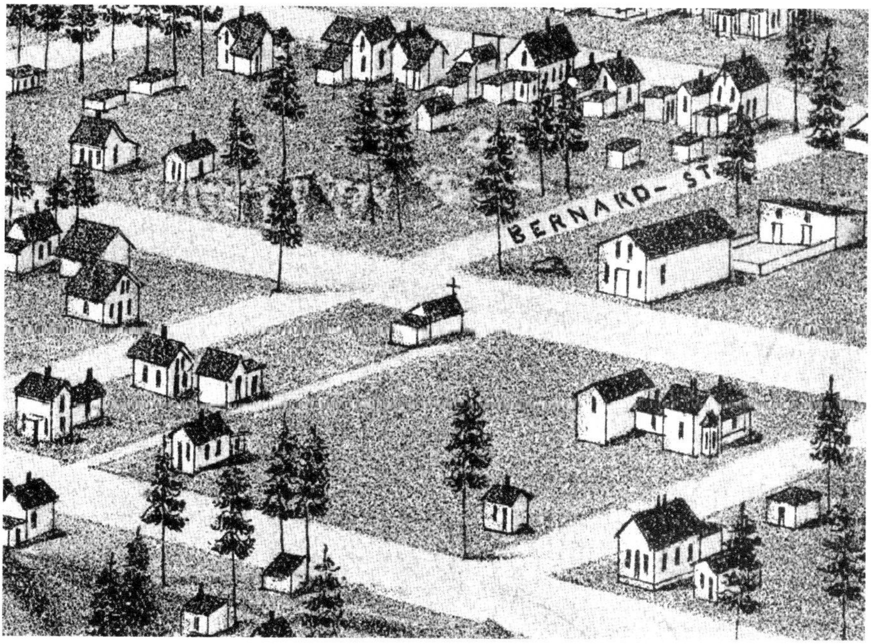

Spokane's first Catholic church (*center*). *Courtesy of Eastern Washington State Historical Society: Museum of Arts and Culture.*

was to get acquainted with the people of Spokane by visiting them in their homes. That summer, she spent countless hours doing whatever she could for the sick and the poor, regardless of their religion. She made many friends that summer and gained an understanding of how the hospital could serve Spokane. She found so much joy in her work that when she finished helping to found three other hospitals, she went back to Spokane and spent the final years of her life welcoming patients and visitors to the hospital.

A few weeks after the Sisters Joseph arrived in Spokane, two nurses came to join their team. Sister Joseph of Arimathea left one recruit in charge of nursing the poor in the city, while she took the other one on a trip into railroad camps and mining towns throughout Eastern Washington and North Idaho, all the while making new friends and finding supporters.

The nuns' success depended heavily on their own ability to raise money. Years earlier Mother Joseph had developed a way to finance her projects. The motherhouse in Montreal could not have raised enough for all the regional houses. Instead, Mother Joseph had repeatedly traveled across the Pacific Northwest on tours, called "begging trips." When she and her associates arrived in Spokane, they had already visited countless pioneer settlements across the region asking for money.

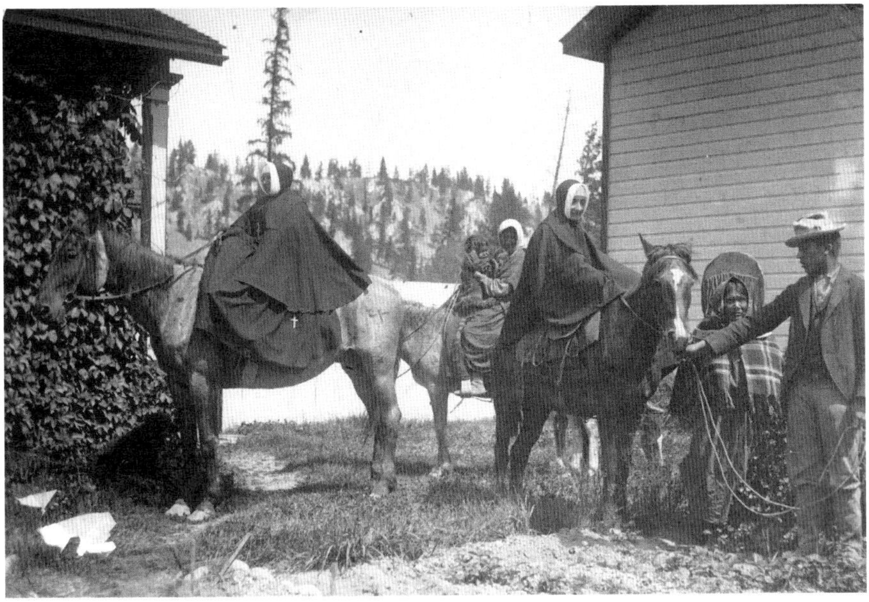

A begging tour the Sisters of Providence took in 1894. *Courtesy of Providence Archives.*

On begging trips, the nuns rode on horseback. Traveling with experienced guides, they toured Washington, Idaho and beyond. In North Idaho, they pulled mining gear over their robes and headed underground, soliciting small sums from miners and accepting other useful goods.

After one such trip, Mother Joseph tried to board a train with a cow in tow. The conductor asked her to purchase a ticket for the animal, but she insisted that her own ticket allowed her to bring a guest. Folklore says the animal got a free ride.

Clearly, Mother Joseph knew how to get things done. Spokane's hospital would soon be another finished project on the growing list of her accomplishments. She now let others raise money and knock on doors while she busied herself with buying property, purchasing wood and bricks, hiring employees, digging a basement and laying a foundation. There was no time to waste.

She sometimes clashed with Sister Joseph of Arimathea, the fundraiser and designated head of the new hospital. At first, Sister Joseph tried to supervise the money spent on construction. Mother Joseph was so irritated by her meddling that she wrote a letter of complaint to their corporate headquarters.

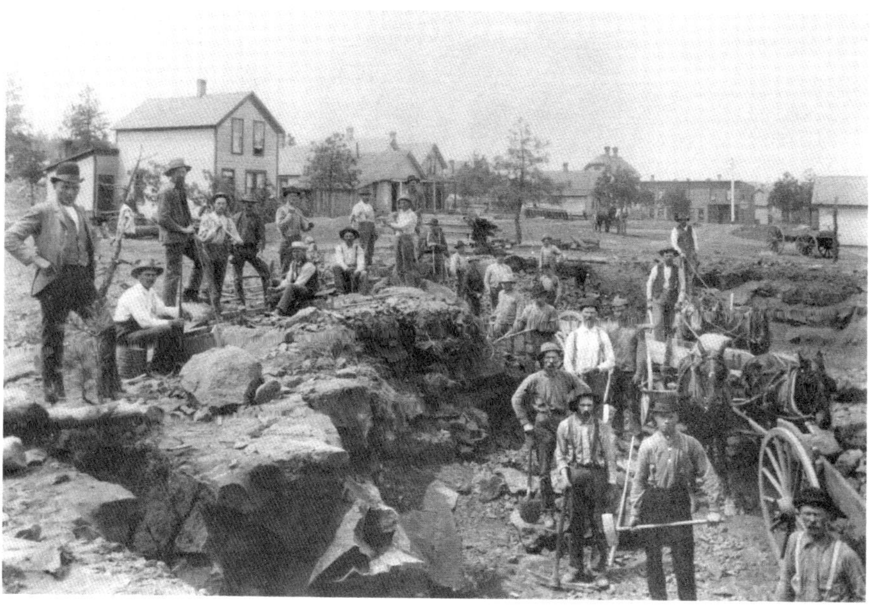

A construction crew on Riverside similar to the one Mother Joseph supervised. *Courtesy of the Ned M. Barnes Northwest Room, Spokane Public Library.*

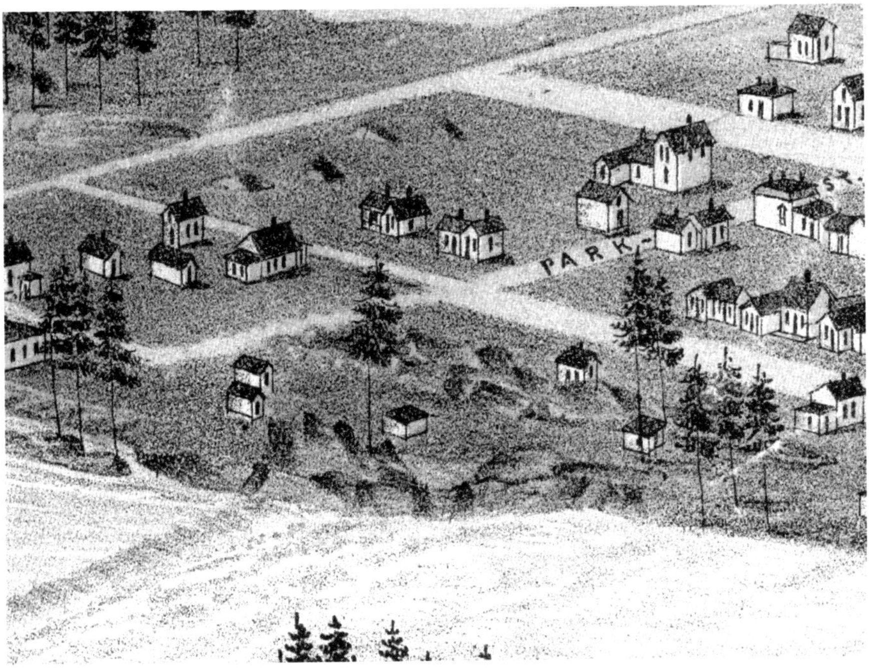

The property Mother Joseph selected for her hospital. *Courtesy of the Eastern Washington State Historical Society: Museum of Arts and Culture.*

On Friday, July 2, only two months after they had arrived in Spokane, Mother Joseph had a completed foundation. By coincidence, she was ready to lay the hospital's cornerstone at the same time that the new Catholic church, Our Lady of Lourdes, was being dedicated. The regional bishop, Father Junger, who was coming to officiate over the church's celebration, could bless the hospital at the same time.

The Sisters of Providence's property covered an area roughly 263 feet wide and 447 feet long. It was big enough that it could easily have housed three more buildings of the same size. Still, the intended size of the hospital, outlined by the newly laid foundation, promised to become the biggest building that Spokane had erected to date. Mother Joseph's plans impressed Spokane's residents and looked especially promising to all who attended the ceremony that day.

A large crowd watched as the tall and portly Bishop Junger, stately in his robes, walked around the foundation's perimeter, bestowing blessings on each side. Then the bishop turned to Mother Joseph and asked, "What is the name of your hospital?"

Mother Joseph caught her breath, thinking with embarrassment that there had not been time to receive a proper name from Montreal. Much to her relief, an assistant priest standing nearby replied smoothly, "It will be Sacred Heart Hospital."

Sacred Heart Hospital was a good name. It commemorated the feast that local Catholics were celebrating that day, but more importantly, it honored the architect and builder. When she had joined the Sisters of Providence, Esther Pariseau had assumed the name Joseph of the Sacred Heart.

Having the hospital named in her honor was gratifying, but Mother Joseph kept her sights on building the hospital and quickly went back to work. Using the shack where the sisters slept each night as an office, the nun, with a hammer in her belt, remained on-site most of the time. She was a skilled and tireless taskmaster who monitored workers closely. She inspected their progress at night. Using a lighted lantern, she even walked on the rafters, bouncing from time to time to check their strength. Once she tore apart a brick chimney so she could rebuild it to a higher standard.

Mother Joseph could do anything she put her hand to, but those who knew her personally also understood that she had a quick and fiery temper. She would ruthlessly confront workers who failed to meet her standards. But when she had cooled off, her better nature would soon return, and her apologies were heartfelt.

Bishop Junger and Father Cataldo appreciated Mother Joseph's talents. Cataldo put his best efforts into Spokane, creating his flagship school, Gonzaga, there. On the other hand, the bishop had asked Mother Joseph to build a school in Sprague, a community southwest of Spokane. He wanted the school there to complement his newly erected Mary Queen of Heaven Church.

Cataldo and Junger had put their bets on two different cities. At the time, Sprague boasted a large hotel and a railroad station where westbound trains from Spokane stopped to fill their boilers with water. A year before, Junger had pushed to erect a beautiful Catholic church there. On the other hand, Cataldo had been aiming to build a school in Spokane for five years.

In support of Junger, Mother Joseph agreed to manage the construction of a three-story wooden school in Sprague, to be named St. Joseph's Academy. It was ready for occupancy before Sacred Heart Hospital was completed. Sister Joseph of Arimathea and the nurses furnished it. Shortly thereafter, two nuns from Vancouver arrived to teach, and the school opened for business on January 6, 1887. It was the first boarding school in Lincoln County, and despite Sprague's steady decline in population, it kept its doors open to students until 1965.

In early January 1887, Spokane residents were eagerly awaiting the opening of Sacred Heart Hospital. The *Spokane Falls Review* pronounced it "one of the most perfect buildings from the point of utility ever constructed." What is more, it had great architectural beauty, with its "lofty cupola" towering above and its verandas overlooking an "enchanting view" of the Spokane River. Estimating that it had cost $20,000, the writer went on to marvel that as recently as the previous spring, not even a shot had been fired into the stone to begin digging its basement.

Spokane's new hospital boasted the latest technology. Its basement held a boiler with two large furnaces that fueled a state-of-the-art hot water heating system. To carry the warmth throughout the hospital, twelve thousand feet of pipe had been installed by a Portland-based company. In addition, the building featured two flush toilets on each floor and a dumbwaiter that extended from the basement to the roof. The stairways were broad with spacious landings, and the interior boasted a built-in sprinkler system in case of fire. Mother Joseph's hospital would open as the most modern building in Spokane.

Six months after laying the cornerstone, the nurses were inside the hospital seeing to last-minute details. They heard a knock at the door, and Sister

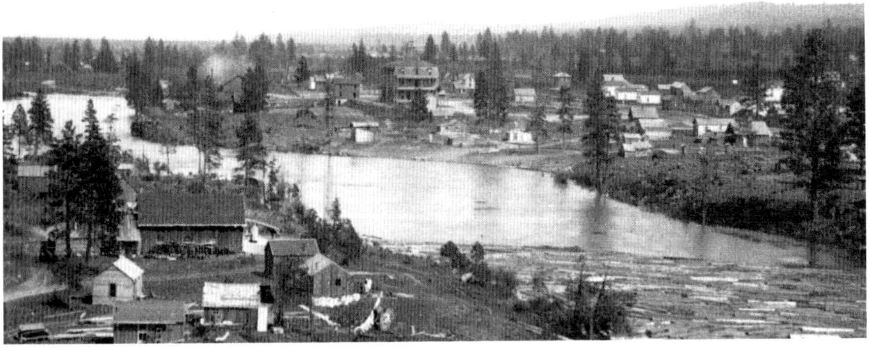

Sacred Heart Hospital, at the center of the far bank, circa 1888. *Courtesy of the Eastern Washington State Historical Society: Museum of Arts and Culture.*

Joseph of Arimathea opened it, finding two charitable women with a man who was extremely ill. The nuns hastily cleared out one of the six operating rooms and prepared a bed for him. The young man was grateful for the sisters' warmth and care, but his illness progressed. He died four days later, becoming both the hospital's first patient and its first death.

Ironically, the hospital's next patient was Mother Joseph, who had been injured by a fall in the cellar. Suddenly, she, too, needed hospital care. For three long weeks, the nun with the hammer in her belt chafed at being unable to work as she lay in the hospital that she had designed.

Twelve days after the death of their first patient, the sisters officially moved in, and the hospital's thirty beds were opened to patients. This modern hospital was ready to provide the care that the nuns had come to Spokane to offer. Sister Joseph of Arimathea launched the tradition she would be remembered for, graciously welcoming any sick or hungry person who came to their door. Years later, a reporter reminisced that Sacred Heart Hospital transformed the town into a city.

2

THREE Rs PLUS MUSIC

The Sisters of Holy Names of Jesus and Mary (SNJM) were next on Cataldo's list to bring to Spokane. They had already distinguished themselves as educators, both in establishing schools and in teaching music. Father Cataldo had been asking them to come for more than five years—much as he had been asking the Sisters of Providence—but they had been hesitant to spread their order thin to cover yet one more mission.

It was never easy for a motherhouse to add a new mission to its works. For one thing, it required paying for additional travel expenses. For another, and perhaps most significantly, it meant the motherhouse had to part with the workers who would go to the new site. For these reasons, the mother superior looked askance at the proposal.

However, people in Spokane were smoothing the path for the nuns to come and teach. Local Catholic parishioners, including the pioneering merchants James Monaghan and M.M. Cowley and their families, helped to raise money for the nuns. The Irish-born Cowley had been an early trader at a post near the Idaho border. His friend James Monaghan sold and shipped goods from Chewelah, a community about fifty miles to the northwest of Spokane Falls.

By the mid-1880s, the Monaghan family lived in Spokane, and both James and his wife, Margaret, were active in Spokane's Catholic community. A mother of five, Margaret especially wanted to bring a Catholic school to town. In December 1887, she and her friends joined the nurses from Sacred Heart in holding a four-day fair. They sold handcrafted items, artwork, household supplies and food, along with items donated by local merchants.

The fair raised $2,000. The nurses at Sacred Heart took half the profits and left the rest to the community, which now had $1,000 for a parochial school.

In February 1888, only a year after Sacred Heart opened its doors, Mother Superior Jean Baptist (SNJM) traveled to Vancouver, Washington, where the Sisters of Providence had their regional headquarters. The superior there gave her guest a glowing report about Sacred Heart Hospital, describing the good it was already doing, and urged her to reconsider her decision not to send a team of educators to Spokane.

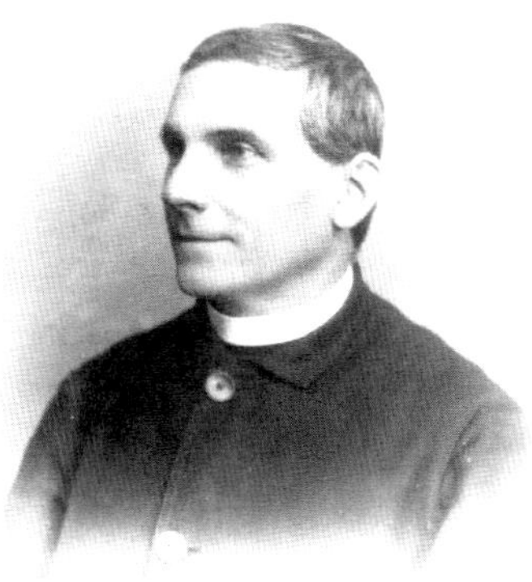

Father Joseph Cataldo, circa 1890, founder of Gonzaga University, invited several orders of nuns to Spokane. *Courtesy of the Ned M. Barnes Northwest Room, Spokane Public Library.*

A few days later, Mother Jean Baptist was in Spokane, looking around the city with Joseph Cataldo and the parish priest, Jame Rebmann. She also toured Sacred Heart Hospital and met the nurses. The up-to-date hospital and new Catholic church nearby helped give the city a polished look, and the mother superior was impressed enough to change her mind.

Six months later, a team of three SNJM teachers traveled up the coast from California to Washington. After a short visit with the Sisters of Providence in Vancouver, they took the lengthy overland trip to Spokane. Father Rebmann graciously welcomed them and then escorted them around the city in his new "Brewster Buggy." When the tour was over, the priest tied the buggy to a light pole in front of the church. The group went inside, planning to participate in late-afternoon worship services.

Doing his best to give them a favorable impression of Spokane, Rebmann had planned to conduct a solemn worship service in the beauty of the recently built church. It was a hot day, so he left the front door ajar to let some fresh air blow in. The nuns sat reverently in the pews. The priest had just donned his robes and picked up his sermon when, without warning, loud swearing broke the stillness of the moment.

Irritated by the rude intrusion into the quiet serenity, Father Rebmann hurried out the main door. There he found his dog, Karo, which he had tied behind his buggy, growling through bared teeth. Just out of the dog's reach, a man stood rubbing his leg and sending loud profanities into the quiet afternoon. The priest asked the man what had happened. He replied, "I was walking by the church, and noticed that your horse's rein had slipped down the light pole. I stopped to pull it back up, and then your dog bit my leg."

Finding no breaks in the man's skin, only red marks, the irritated priest informed the man that "there had been no bite at all." Adjusting his horse's reins, he sent the man on his way and then went quietly back into the church and began preparing once again to officiate over the service.

Just as the priest was finally beginning the worship service, he was again interrupted, this time by shouts and gunshots outside. Fearing for their lives, the nuns quickly ducked below the pews. Crouched below the pews, they wondered what kind of a city they had come to.

Father Rebmann ran back outside to see his frightened horse pulling its driverless buggy over the bridge, heading toward home—Gonzaga's stables. On another street, a gun-toting policeman chased Karo. The man who had been bit and a group of boys followed him, yelling "mad dog." The policeman shot again and again, missing Karo as he ran.

Chagrined that his peaceful service had been interrupted by the chaos on the streets, Father Rebmann gathered his wits about him and proceeded with the service, only to be interrupted one last time. A worried stable hand from Gonzaga rushed in to check on the priest. He had seen the panicked horse with the driverless buggy careening into the stables. The sweating horse, cushions askew and missing lap robe and whip convinced the man that something serious had happened to the priest. Frightened, he ran all the way into town.

When it was all over, the nuns had a good laugh and breathed a sigh of relief; they had had a taste of Spokane's wild side. They would remember the incident, passing the story on to their successors for generations to come.

Despite the occasional chaotic moment, the newest nuns enjoyed more comforts than Mother Joseph had. The SNJM women stayed as guests at Sacred Heart Hospital until the construction of their school was completed. They had plenty to tell the nurses at Sacred Heart that night, and their hosts had many stories of their own to tell about their adopted city.

Located on Main Street, next to Our Lady of Lourdes Church, their school was within a half mile of the city center. Most students walked to school. The building was not fancy; it did not sport a lofty cupola on top, but it was roomy enough to house the sisters and their students.

The teachers were as excited about the beginning of school as the children were. On September 3, 1888, the secretary happily wrote, "At last the day has

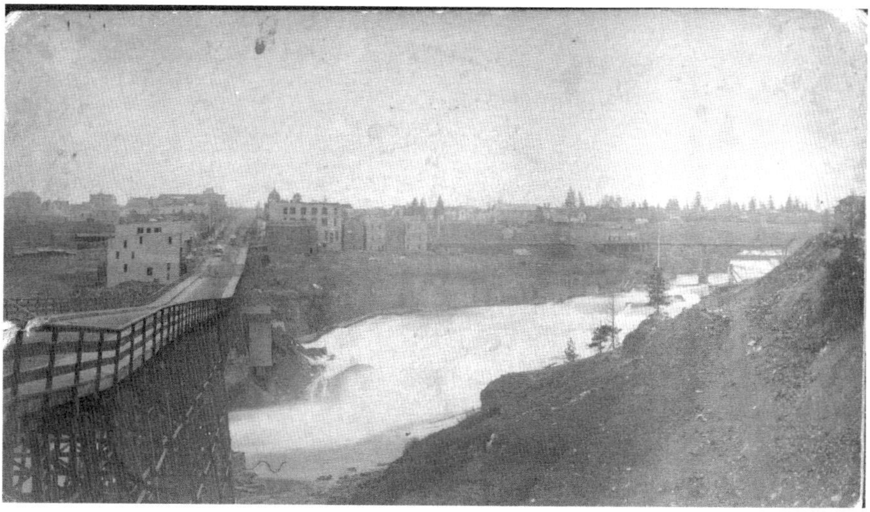

First Monroe Street Bridge. *Courtesy of Ned M. Barnes Room Northwest Room, Spokane Public Library.*

arrived when we can welcome students to our school." They admitted girls first. Two days later, after the girls were settling into a routine, the teachers opened the school to boys. The boys would study in different classrooms and go outside for separate recesses. Experienced teachers, the sisters knew how to make two schools work in one building.

In addition to teaching the three Rs, many of the SNJM sisters were accomplished musicians. They always included music lessons in their curriculum. Thus, their students could learn to play instruments and sing at the same time that they learned the basics of reading, writing and 'rithmetic.

When the imposing Bishop Junger arrived in Spokane in late October, the students and teachers were enjoying their new routines. Our Lady of Lourdes was packed with family and friends, there to watch 150 happy students parade from the school through the open doors and walk to the front of the church. A girl named Mary welcomed the priest and guests.

Bishop Junger was impressed by the performance. He congratulated the students on their good behavior, stressing how much they had learned and challenging them to continue studying all they could. The sheer number of students was impressive, and the music they performed demonstrated a skill that would become the trademark for the order that still is evident today. Holy Names School was off to a great start.

3

FIRE!

It was hot on the afternoon of August 4, 1889. Harriet Ross was relaxing on her front porch, looking over the city that lay to the south. The heat was so oppressive that she had gone outside looking for air movement. Her dress clumped around her legs, but the hot, dry wind gave little comfort. Neighborhood dogs twitched their tails and slept uneasily under whatever shade they could find.

The traditional late summer dryness had begun weeks early. News of fires had filled the papers. Stagecoach routes had been canceled and blackened Ponderosa pine trees looked like tall skeletons on the nearby hills and mountains. Clouds of choking smoke settled near the ground, coloring the houses and buildings several shades darker than they already were. Dust wafted through the air, stirred by the hooves of passing horses and buggy wheels. Heating the air still more, trains moved in and out of the city on four different rail lines.

At 6:00 p.m., a cookstove in a rooming house on Railroad Avenue between Post and Lincoln Streets caught fire. No one thought too much of it when a small flame went through the roof of the house. A few buckets of water and a brigade should be able to put it out. Ross watched the volunteer fire department arrive and quickly hook hoses to the city's new fire hydrants. The volunteers stepped back, expecting gushes of water. But nothing came out. The pumps had no water pressure.

Ross, whose porch offered a perfect observation point, soon welcomed other ladies who lived nearby. The friends watched with horror as a flaming roof on the west side of the city fell into a rooming house, and a sudden strong wind picked up the fire, taking it to the building across the street. Soon the fire raged east along Spokane's main streets.

Safe on the north side of the river, the ladies watched as chaos spread until the fire covered six square blocks of downtown. It raced from one dry wooden building to the next in the blink of an eye, even burning valuables that desperate residents had placed in the middle of the streets in hopes of saving them. A steady stream of loaded wagons struggled across the bridges and sped north, up and away from the fire. Another line of heavy wagons snaked up the South Hill.

Screams of frightened people and animals intermingled with the booms of exploding dynamite. Volunteers were systematically blowing up corner buildings, hoping to create breaks that would stop the fire. The spaces left in the wake of the explosions provided room for more wind, which merely helped the fire along. It kept burning until 9:00 p.m., when the winds, and the fire along with them, finally died. All the banks, hotels and large businesses, along with the land and post offices, were gone. Thirty-six blocks of Spokane's downtown were flattened. A heavy blanket of air and an eerie silence lingered through the night.

The massive destruction forever etched itself on Harriet's mind. She and her husband, A.J. Ross, had lived in the city for several years. They

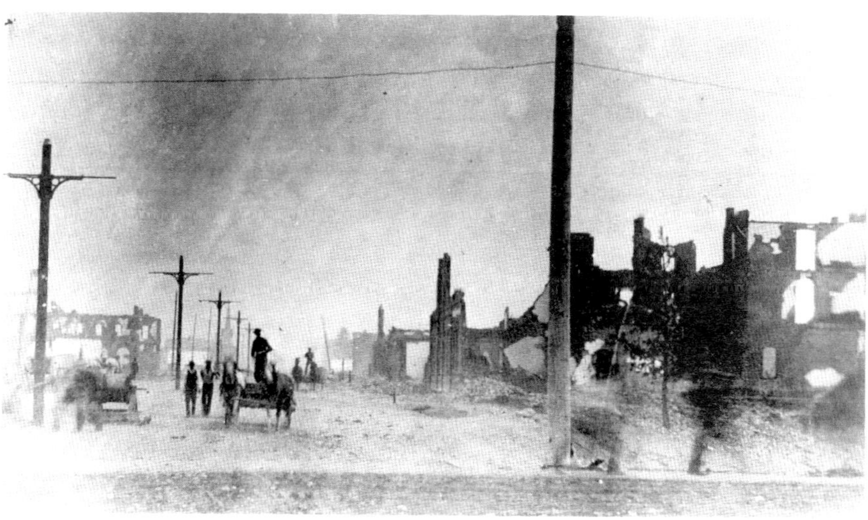

This photo taken shortly after the fire shows both the devastation and efforts to rebuild. *Courtesy of the Ned M. Barnes Northwest Room, Spokane Public Library.*

had developed Ross Park, the first neighborhood built on the north side of the river. To service it, they created the city's first streetcar line, designed to take buyers from their homes on the north side to Spokane's business district. Watching the stores and hotels of her chosen hometown disappear in a span of four hours was both fascinating and devastating for Harriet.

Ross and her friends had already been looking for ways to help Spokane residents. They were especially interested in the plight of disadvantaged women and children. Their quest to help the poor in Spokane had begun in December 1886, when a group of women had organized a ball and raised $145.80 for the relief of the poor.

In January 1887, the ladies had met in their favorite hat shop to discuss the best way to use the money. They established the Ladies' Benevolent Society, created a constitution and elected officers. By the time of the fire, they had established a three-member relief committee, charged with visiting Spokane's poorest in their homes. The ladies would report back to the full committee; then the group would purchase groceries, befriend lonely widows and tend to those who were ill. They also taught poor children how to sew and threw parties and balls.

The charitable ladies looked for families crowded into single rooms, whose members often included small children. Besides being hungry and in need of clothing, sometimes these people became ill. When they did, the ladies would employ a physician or nurse. At times, they would even take the sick person out of the home, placing him or her at Sacred Heart Hospital.

When sick parents were bedridden, they had difficulty caring for their children. In such situations, the ladies looked for alternative living arrangements for the children. They believed they were doing the children a favor by taking them out of their crowded and disease-ridden homes.

In an era before foster care and with no orphanages in the city, the charitable ladies were filling a need. But the work was not easy. It was often difficult to find residents who were both willing and able to take a poor child into their home. In the months before the fire, Ross and her friends had been considering creating a hospital, or home, in which they could provide care for those who were poor, sick or orphaned.

It would be a big job, but these ladies had connections to the leading developers and investors in Spokane. Moreover, many were members of local Protestant churches; they could easily gain the support of their congregations. In fact, the organization they created was large enough that the ladies believed it would relieve individual churches of the responsibility of establishing their own charitable groups.

Then the 1889 fire swept through downtown Spokane. As they sat on Harriet Ross's porch and watched the destruction rising in the wake of the fire, the ladies realized many more people would be needing help. They knew they had to get busier.

4
CREATING A CHARITY

In the days immediately following the fire, Ross and her friends resolved to focus more effort on getting their own building. They had been holding meetings in one of the YMCA's rooms. Having a building to work from would save them the expense of sending their patients to the hospital, give them space for meetings and provide rooms to care for the needy.

The ladies had assisted one hundred people during the previous year, and they planned to increase that number in 1890. With a building to bring their meetings and their work together, they figured they could accomplish a lot more than they had in any previous year.

The plan to build fell into place more easily after the fire. Boosters were beginning new construction projects almost as soon as the last flames had been extinguished. The flow of money into town also made it easier for the ladies to raise money.

Some individuals still had money to donate. J.J. Browne gave the ladies a tract of land valued at $3,000. It lay approximately one mile north of the river, surrounded by the property that he and his fellow boosters were developing for new homes.

J.J. Browne was one of Spokane's four founders. He had homesteaded 120 acres along the river near the falls and then continued to purchase property, selling smaller portions to newcomers. One of the city's first upscale neighborhoods, Browne's Addition, was named in his honor.

In October 1889, Anna Stratton Browne, wife of J.J. and a founding member of the Ladies' Benevolent Society, devoted several afternoons to

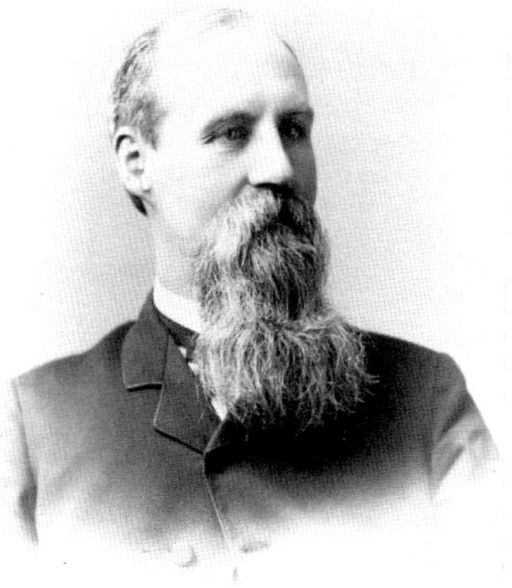

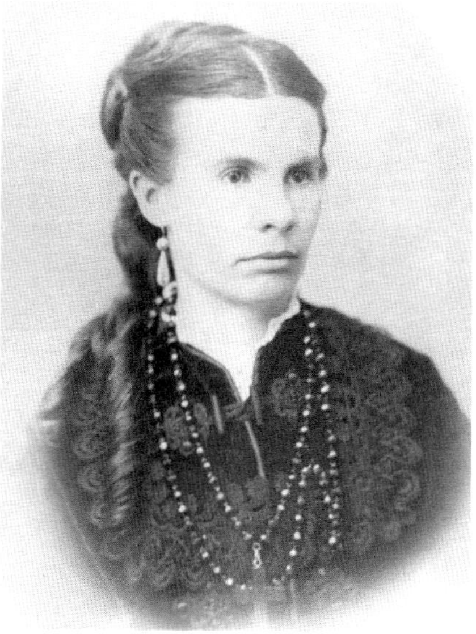

Left: J.J. Browne, one of the four founders of Spokane and husband of Anna Stratton Browne. *Courtesy of the Ned M. Barnes Northwest Room, Spokane, Public Library.*

Right: Anna Stratton Browne, a member of the Ladies' Benevolent Society, remained active in women's clubs through the turn of the twentieth century. *Courtesy of the Eastern Washington State Historical Society, Museum of Arts and Culture.*

raising money. After four days, she had collected more than $2,000, or 10 percent of the club women's goal.

In the days following the fire, money and goods had poured in to city coffers from concerned individuals, as well as from Seattle, Portland and other cities. Spokane's city council soon controlled $34,000 that was to be distributed by one of the city's leading citizens and the relief committee.

Since they had released donors from pledges made before the fire, the charitable ladies set their eyes on the relief money. They had personal and professional ties with city council members, which helped them gain the attention of city leaders. Only two weeks after the fire, the women happily accepted $1,000 in official funds.

The city relief committee also presented $500 to the nurses at Sacred Heart Hospital. Since the fire, the nuns had been treating injured people and feeding the homeless. The money helped defray the expenses of their ongoing work.

The $1,500 for women's charities was part of Spokane's initiative to address the needs that had arisen since the fire. In the first month, the city distributed over $6,000 in free meals, cash, supplies and outbound train tickets. Local leaders encouraged indigents who had family or friends elsewhere to go join them. City commissioners liked that approach because it reduced the number of needy people in town.

The Ladies' Benevolent Society had difficulty deciding how to spend the $1,000. It was not enough to pay for the building they wanted, and it did not cover the gap between the money they had raised and what they needed to finish the project. They soon decided to seek more money. The ladies wanted to establish both a hospital and a home.

They felt a sense of urgency. If they established a hospital quickly, they could get all the county patients who were then being cared for at Sacred Heart. A county commissioner had hinted that they could do so. Buoyed by the idea, the ladies worked with renewed energy.

On November 2, 1889, they attended a special meeting of the city's relief committee with Mayor Pratt. The group met to consider requests for money and to decide how the relief funds could best be used. They talked to the women about their plan and then passed a unanimous resolution to give up to $8,500 to help the women build a home. The council members endorsed their plan, believing the ladies had such good moral characters that any charity they developed would be effective in helping the destitute families living in the city.

On November 8, the ladies took their architectural drawings to the city council for approval. The committee adopted the plans and asked the architect to prepare the plans so the ladies could begin accepting bids to build the home. It would be three stories high and have a basement. A temporary building, it was designed for the back of the lot, leaving room for a larger building to be placed there in the future.

On November 15, a short announcement appeared in the paper reporting that a temporary home for the friendless would be started immediately. Anna Stratton Browne and Harriet Ross were to be in charge of it.

In the meantime, the ladies rented a house and began taking in homeless people, as well as providing medical help to those who needed it. A local benefactor paid the rent for one month, and a physician donated his services. At the same time, the ladies were operating a Saturday afternoon industrial school for poor girls, teaching them needlepoint along with some reading and writing.

The ladies' decision to establish a hospital seemed natural at the time. In fact, in the three years since Sacred Heart had opened its doors, several more hospitals had been established. In local jargon, the nuns operated

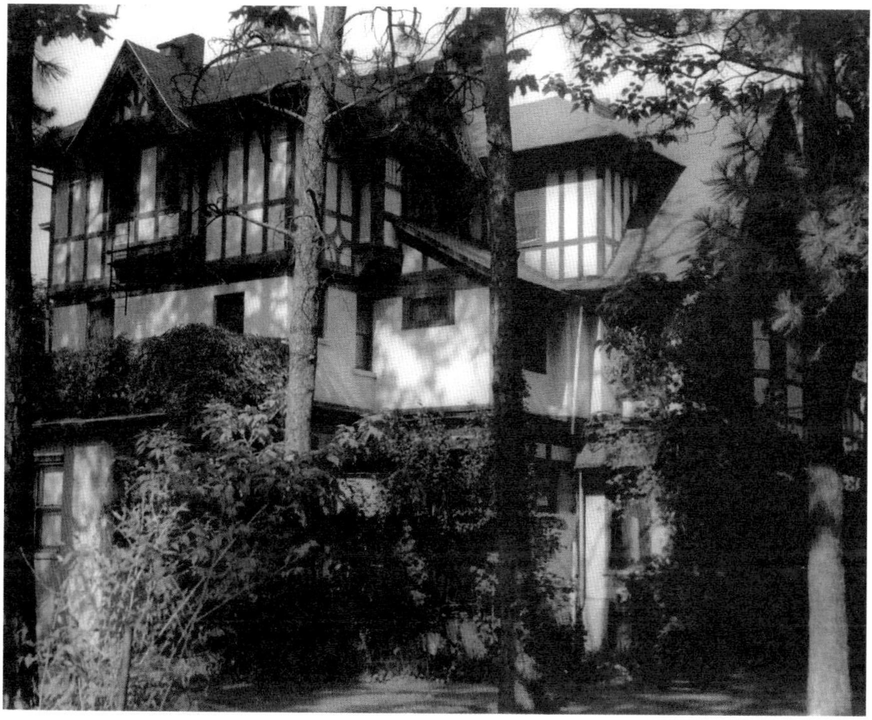

J.J. and Anna Stratton Browne's home in Browne's Addition. *Courtesy of the Ned M. Barnes Room, Spokane Public Library.*

"the Catholic" one. A Protestant version had its doors open by 1890. Donors from the eastern United States had recently contributed $10,000 for an Episcopalian infirmary, and several thousand dollars were donated in early 1890 to open a Scandinavian facility. This meant that the Home of the Friendless, slated to open its doors in April 1890, would become the fifth hospital in the city.

By mid-February, the club had run out of money. Not only were the ladies paying to build the home, but they also had other charitable cases to tend to, in addition to operating their industrial school. For example, they paid one dollar per day for each patient they placed at Sacred Heart.

Political contests between city and county leaders limited the ladies' income. After the fire relief committee had given so much money to the ladies' building fund, city council members pulled back, refusing to give more for operating expenses. They argued that the county should pay since the city and its commissioners were paying property taxes to the county.

In recent months, county commissioners had paid $640 of the charity's bills. But that was not enough, and on February 19, the ladies asked the city council for $600 to help them pay more bills. Council members responded by asking the relief committee for a donation from leftover money from that fund. Getting $500 that way was much less painful than taking money away from ongoing city business.

By April, the home was nearly complete. A large edifice that locals predicted would be a credit to Spokane, it was a three-story building with a double front door, covered with an arch. The interior would be equipped with excellent waterworks and two mammoth furnaces that could heat the entire building with both gas and electricity. It would feature a dining hall, a kitchen with a commodious closet, a reception area, a large room for the matron, two hospital wards and a room for elderly women. It would be completed with a first-class laundry, nursery and apartments for servants and have hard pine floors.

On May 22, the society dedicated Spokane's Home of the Friendless. The doors were open throughout the day, and guests could explore the various

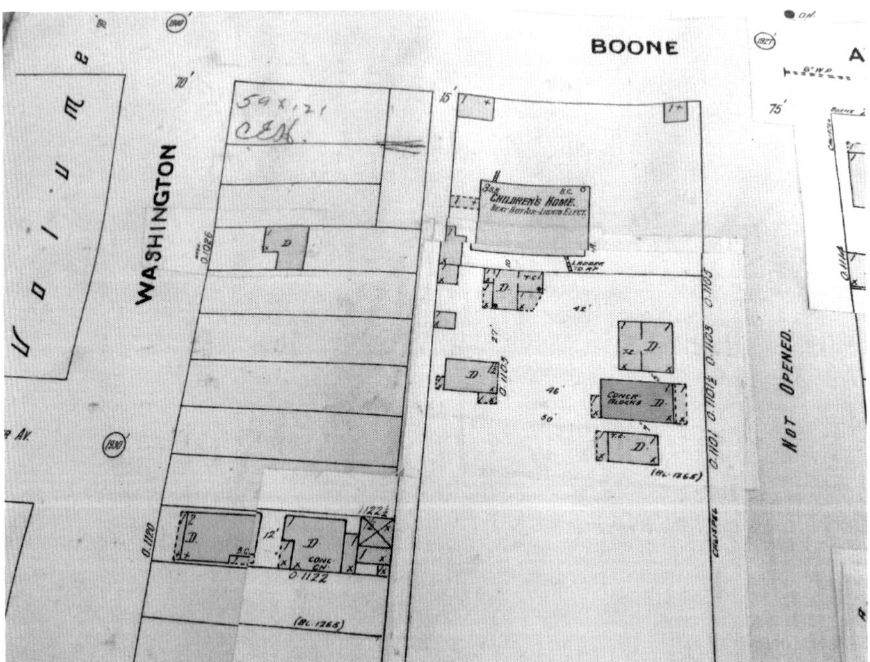

This piece of an 1890 Sanborn Map shows the home's footprint, labeled Children's Home. *Courtesy of the Ned M. Barnes Northwest Room, Spokane Public Library.*

rooms and admire the donated furnishings. Six churches—two Methodist, a Unitarian, a Christian, a Congregational and an Episcopal—had taken on the task of furnishing different rooms with tables, chairs, beds, carpets, draperies and paintings.[1]

At 3:00 p.m., the ladies, their invited guests and an orchestra assembled in the parlor for a formal dedication. After music and a prayer, Mary Todd presented a history of the Ladies' Benevolent Society, going back to a Mother Goose Charity Ball held in December 1886. Since then, she reported, they had helped 660 people by providing food and clothing, nursing the sick, occasionally paying for rent or travel tickets and hiring 21 nurses to tend to their charges. Their organization, she added, had grown to include 163 members.

Todd and another club lady, several Protestant ministers, two judges and at least one of Spokane's founding fathers spoke during the service. A.M. Cannon, chair of the city's fire relief committee, presented the ladies with a check for $2,000. The Reverend May C. Jones, Spokane's first woman pastor, offered a touching benediction.

Nine months after the fire of August 1889 and only five months after Washington Territory became a state, the ladies had their own building: Spokane's Home of the Friendless. Its presence tied Spokane to other urban cities throughout the United States where activist women worked to help the poor. Spokane's version, overlooking Bernard Street, enjoyed broad support in the city. Ross, Todd and their friends had done what they set out to do.

5
HOSPITAL OR HOME?

Mary Todd and the other members of the Ladies' Benevolent Society aimed for the Home of the Friendless to become a model institution. They expected their home to be smoothly run, well-funded and respected throughout the city.

A prominent member of the society's relief committee, Todd had visited homes where she had seen starving babies and had talked to sick mothers and grandmothers who were barely able to care for themselves, let alone help their children. She had tended to sick young women and men who were alone in the city with no money.

For example, during the winter of 1890, she took Annie Olsen, a recent immigrant and a domestic servant, under her wing. Olsen became so sick that Todd escorted her to Sacred Heart Hospital. The unfortunate young woman died a few days later, and her story might have ended quietly at the hospital if she had been buried quickly and efficiently.

But Todd, who was not at the hospital when Olsen died, told an undertaker to ask the city to pay for her burial. She later chose not to attend Olsen's funeral, excusing herself because the weather had turned bitterly cold. Two days after, she was horrified to find Olsen's mutilated body at a competing undertaker's shop, insufficiently clad and still unburied.

She and the Benevolent Ladies took the story to the press. They accused the undertaker of negligence and unlawful mutilation of the body and implied that the nuns at Sacred Heart Hospital had lost Annie's three nightgowns, in addition to leaving her to a lonely death. The whole

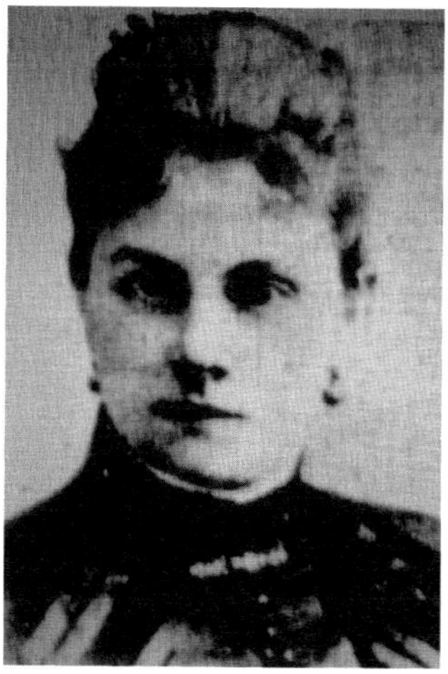

Mary K. Todd, early president of the Ladies' Benevolent Society. *Courtesy of the* Spokesman Review.

situation, however, might have been avoided if Todd had remained informed about Olsen's condition or had at least chosen, when she did find out that the young lady had died, to help with funeral arrangements.

Todd's indifference to Olsen made the Ladies' Benevolent Society look uncaring, but Todd apologized to a sympathetic reporter, who then publicized her side of the story. He informed Spokane readers that the undertakers were to blame.

The newspaper story helped focus the city's attention on the man who claimed to be a doctor and had dissected Olsen's body. He had conducted the "autopsy" at an undertaker's office owned by two other men. The State of Washington formally charged the three men with mutilating Annie Olsen's body. In the end, the doctor and one of the undertakers went out of business. In the spring of 1890, the three remaining undertakers joined forces, becoming the proprietors of Spokane's only remaining undertaking business.

Todd excused her own role in the tragedy by telling her co-workers that Olsen's case would have been much easier to keep track of if the ladies had been able to care for the ill woman in their own institution. Todd's contention was true to a certain extent, but she was using it to excuse her own negligence. If Olsen had been a daughter or a close friend, Todd would have attended the funeral and seen that the body was properly buried, cold weather or not.

Todd and her friends had high expectations when they dedicated the home in the spring of 1890. The ladies were confident that their new building would help charity work progress much more smoothly. Their home would be so successful, they believed, that they could meet the needs of all the poorest in the city by feeding and caring for them, helping their children learn a trade, providing a place for some to live and nursing the sick.

Optimistically, the ladies began supervising the home. Their broad agenda reflected the range of needs that the club's relief committee members had encountered as they visited in the homes of the poor in Spokane. They opened a room where mothers could drop off their small children and head to a job or to do other business. They hired a matron and nurses to tend the children and the sick and welcomed elderly women who needed a place to call home.

By the end of the summer, Todd and her associates had noticed that the mothers who were dropping off their children each day were women who lived near the home. Since the home was surrounded by newly platted subdivisions, their patrons were not poor. Instead, they were mothers who found it convenient to leave their children while they went out.

The ladies did not want to continue paying someone to watch the children of well-to-do families. So Todd announced to a reporter that they would no longer provide daycare. They would, however, continue to nurse the sick, teach young girls to sew and even house a few orphans.

Thus, in September, less than four months after they had opened their doors, the ladies published a call to remove the children from their nursery. Todd and the other lady managers had learned that caring for children did not mesh with managing hospital wards. It was difficult to find staff who could handle both sick adults and rambunctious children. Besides, the noise the children made could be difficult for patients to tolerate.[2]

The managers chose to narrow the focus of their charity to the hospital. They knew people were moving to the city in record numbers. Trains were bringing new residents into town each week, and with the immigrants came more sick people. It seemed most expedient to create a hospital.

The ladies now had a large building in which to house patients and store supplies. And so, they officially established Spokane's Home Hospital.

6
WHO HELPS THE POOR?

The winter of 1890–91 passed by without incident. The Home Hospital was taking in sick people, half of all the patients the county was paying for. The ladies employed nurses to tend the patients while Todd and her associates met for regular meetings, raised money and administrated the hospital. This arrangement worked smoothly enough for seven months after the ladies had closed their children's department.

Then, in early April, Todd and her associates decided they were ready to care for more patients. In the months since the home had opened, the county poor had been split between Sacred Heart and the Home Hospital. That spring, they decided that the Home Hospital could take over the contract to serve all county patients. They submitted a formal bid to the county to charge seventy-five cents per patient per day, ten cents less per day than the Sisters at Sacred Heart had bid. The Home Hospital won the contract. Todd and her associates finally had all the county patients.[3]

Their building featured seven hospital wards with plenty of space for the patients. But less than three weeks after winning the contract, the ladies quietly informed county commissioners that they wished to be relieved of the contract; thus, the county was free to make other arrangements for the care of the poor. They closed by explaining that they did not have any ill feelings about the patients but had simply decided to run their institution as a home instead of a hospital.[4]

Todd and her associates had no experience in managing a hospital, and they had discovered that it was not an easy task. Their most serious problem

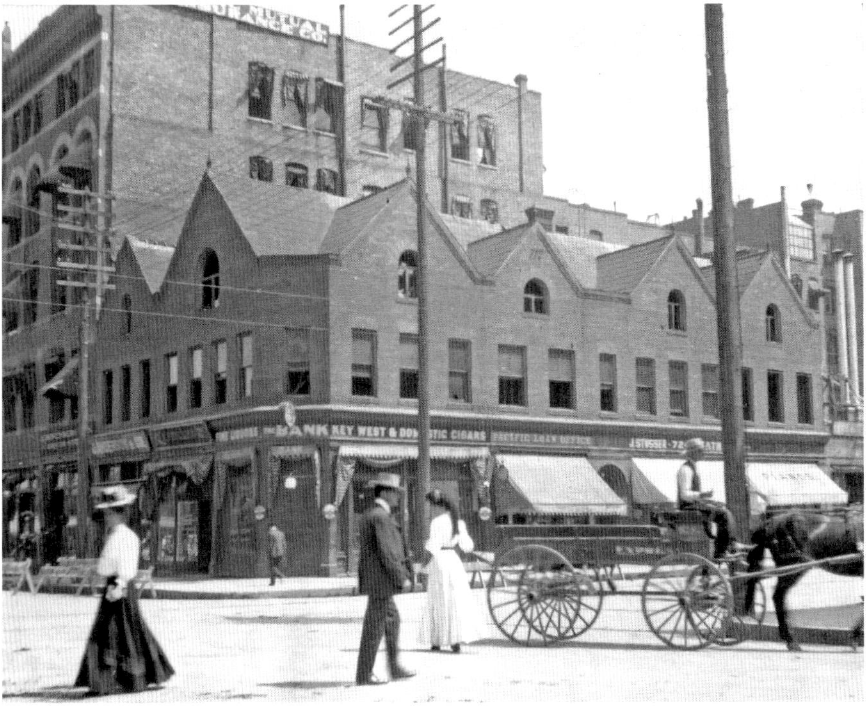

Influential women have played important roles in Spokane since its pioneer days. *Courtesy of the Ned M. Barnes Northwest Room, Spokane Public Library.*

was that they needed a much more dependable water supply than they had. They had hired a contractor to help them dig a deeper well. Six weeks later, the ladies visited a city council meeting.

Todd told the council about the man who was helping sink their well deeper. By early June, they had paid him $300, but their water supply was no better. The contractor had promised he could find water by drilling through solid rock—at the cost of an additional $360. Handing the council chairmen a list of local poor for whom they had cared, the ladies requested more money.

City council members pronounced the ladies' presentation "businesslike." They discussed the expense of caring for the poor; then their conversation wandered into complaining about a pet peeve of theirs—Spokane County's policy of requiring residents to live in the county for six months before receiving assistance. A physician at the meeting reinforced the council members' grievance by stating that in his former job as the city physician, he had met with many new residents who had been unable to get help from the county. Finally, after pulling the conversation back to the Home of the Friendless, council members voted to give the Benevolent Ladies $500.

Todd wrapped up her presentation to the city council with a story about a woman with several children living at 607 East Second Street. The family was in absolute need, and the mother wanted to go to Vancouver, British Columbia, where she thought the father of her children was living. Both the Benevolent Ladies and the members of city council believed that the family would do better if the mother and children could be reunited with the father. However, they had another reason to send the family away: it was cheaper for the city to pay the family's way to Vancouver than to pay the family's rent and provide their food. What they didn't say, but were very cognizant of, was that even if there turned out to be no husband there, the problem of supporting the family would become Vancouver's—instead of Spokane's.

While the ladies who managed the home struggled with the building's water supply, Sacred Heart Hospital was growing. The loss of their patients had been a big challenge for the sisters, but they got them back easily after the ladies released them. The nuns were not strangers to the struggle of keeping their hospital full. During their first years, they had had to look beyond the city limits to miners and residents of nearby Indian reservations. But they kept their doors open. Within months of opening the hospital, Mother Joseph began drawing up plans for an addition. About a year and half after Sacred Heart had opened its doors, the addition was completed and ready for occupancy.

During the same period, Todd and her associates were experiencing ups and downs. They struggled many days with the question of how to design their charity. The home they had created was not instantly stable, though they had begun with high intentions. Todd and her friends had settled one question: Spokane's Home of the Friendless would focus on needy children.

Despite the ladies' indecisiveness, their home would last well into the twentieth century.

7
WHO GETS THE CHILDREN?

While they were going through the process of defining the type of charity the Home of the Friendless would be, Todd and her associates were also participating in a debate over religion in Spokane. The question was which church should be caring for the sick, taking care of needy children and teaching.

Most early hospitals in town were identified by religion. Sacred Heart was known by locals as the Catholic hospital. The Home Hospital, run by the Ladies' Benevolent Society, was a Protestant effort. Private schools and orphanages also divided along denominational lines.

While Todd and her friends were debating about how to define the home, local Catholics had established a school and were taking steps to create an orphanage. For several years, Father Cataldo, the founder of Gonzaga, had been working with other priests in town, including Father Charles Mackin, SJ, to find an order of nuns who would come to help needy children. By late 1889, they were preparing to welcome the Sisters of St. Francis to Spokane to establish an orphanage.

The Benevolent Ladies heard about the Catholic orphanage in the works at about the same time that the Home of the Friendless was under construction. Todd and her friends thought a Catholic orphanage would be a direct threat to their own charity. The matron, an Irish Protestant, summoned Father Mackin and demanded that he cancel his plans to build an orphanage. More moderate ladies, such as Todd, informed him that they were planning to become the city's foremost orphanage and did not think that a similar Catholic institution would help.

But another incident between Mackin and the Benevolent Ladies convinced him to continue with plans for the orphanage. It involved nine German children whose father had been killed in a logging accident. Left with nine children to feed, their mother began looking for a place for the children to stay while she sought employment. She heard about the home and took her children there. The ladies agreed to take the children in, but problems arose when the mother asked the matron to make sure that her children attended Mass. Now Todd and her associates would have been happy to help the children participate in Protestant services—they might even have considered inviting a priest to come to the home. They did invite ministers to visit on Sundays and provide the children with short worship services. But taking children to a Catholic Mass was another matter altogether.

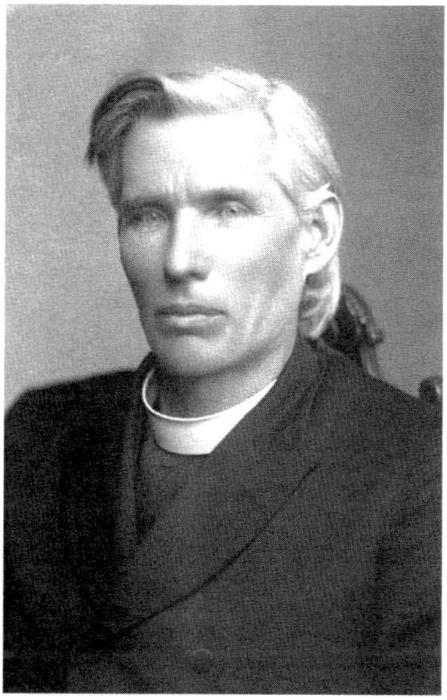

Father Charles Mackin, SJ, a parish priest and the first president of Gonzaga. *Courtesy of Jesuit Archives, Gonzaga University.*

The matron summoned Father Mackin, also a native of Ireland, and insisted that he take all nine children out of the home immediately. Unfortunately, Mackin—who boarded at Gonzaga—had no space for the children. Moreover, there were only a few Catholic families in Spokane at the time. After attempting to locate them nearby, he finally divided the siblings, sending the girls to stay with some nuns in Lewiston, Idaho, and the boys to a school on the Coeur d'Alene reservation at Desmet, Idaho.

The incident with the German children happened some months before the Benevolent Ladies' failed attempt to make their home a hospital. When the ladies decided to shift their emphasis away from patients, they needed more children. They had a very large building, with plenty of room to care for them.

It was one thing to find indigent patients. Both the city and the county were in the business of caring for poor people, and people with illnesses who needed better care were easier to identify. Finding children whom the ladies could help was difficult.

Todd and the other benevolent ladies had connections with a number of Protestant churches in Spokane. Many of the society's members were active in one of the city's Methodist churches. Their pastors could refer children to them. From the beginning, the ladies had worked to gain the support of a variety of Protestant churches, including Christian, Unitarian and Congregational groups, and as they developed their home for children, this network proved valuable.

In addition, Todd admitted young people referred to them by the police department. One fifteen-year-old runaway, Christine, came to the home in June 1891 accompanied by a policeman. A few days after she was settled in the home, her mother and stepfather came looking for her, accompanied by a nurse and a police officer.

Christine looked out a window and saw her family approaching. She panicked. With the matron's approval, Christine raced up six flights of stairs and asked an adult staff member there for help. The woman hid her in a closet and closed the door. Christine eventually emerged when the nurse promised that her parents would not be allowed to take her with them. The parents, nurse and police officer left without the girl.

An hour later, Dr. Mary Latham, Spokane's first woman physician—and on this occasion a messenger for the Catholic Ladies' Benevolent Society—visited the home with a letter signed by the police chief requesting that they place Christine in the doctor's care.

The matron allowed Christine to leave with Latham, thinking the doctor would keep the girl away from her stepfather. She did—for a short time. She kept her away from the sheriff as well, for a few hours. Thirty minutes before the girl was to appear in court, the sheriff came to the home looking for Christine. The matron told him to ask the police chief, who by that time had left work for the day.

Somehow the authorities found Christine. The girl appeared in court that evening. There the presiding judge ruled that she must return to her legal guardians. Rumors suggested that her parents took her to Portland, Oregon, soon after the trial.

Todd and the lady managers lost track of the girl after she was returned to her parents. At the time, state law automatically gave children to their guardians.[5] The best the law could do for an abused minor would be to convict an abusive guardian of an unrelated crime. The charitable ladies understood this and published a call in the newspaper for assistance in bringing the stepfather, who Christine said had tried to strangle her, to justice.

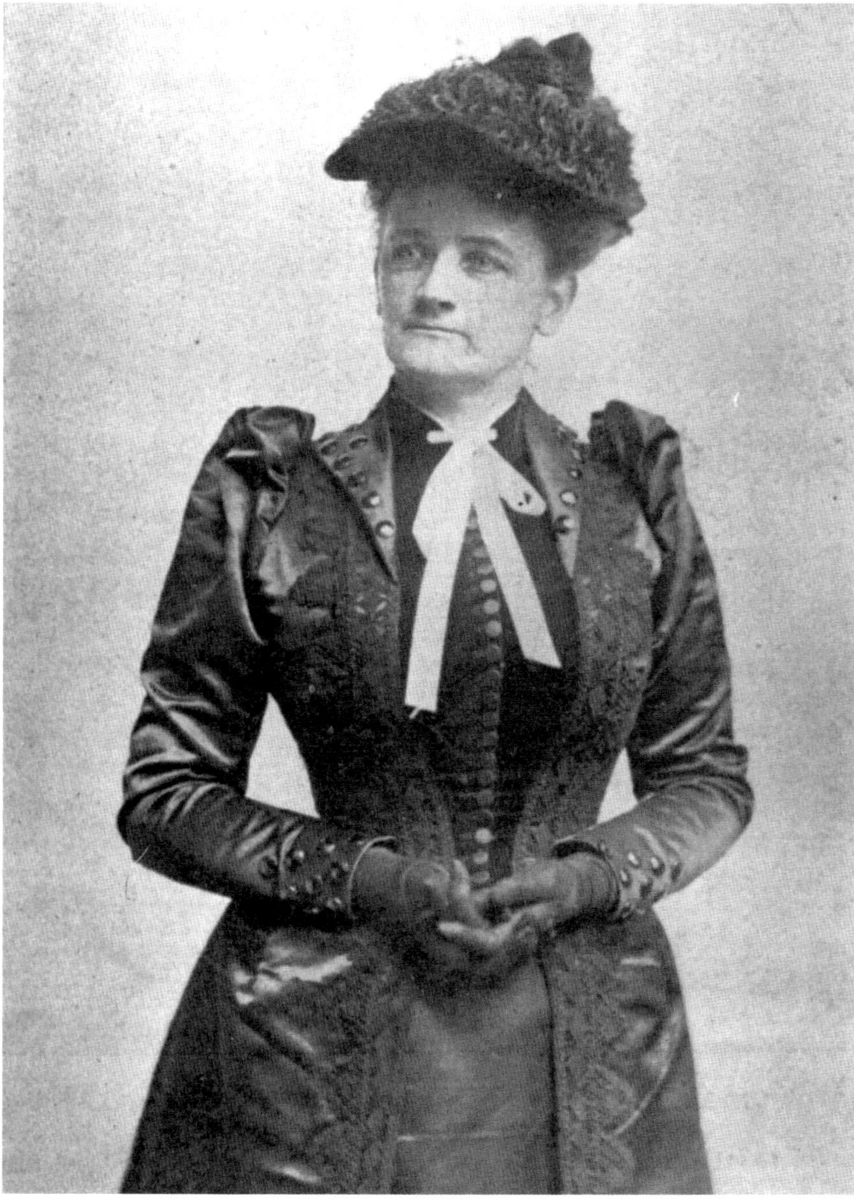

Dr. Mary Latham was Spokane's first female physician. *Courtesy of the Eastern Washington State Regional Archives: Museum of Arts and Culture.*

The Protestant ladies enjoyed the ear of the press, and they got their story about Christine published; it filled several column inches of newspaper space. The immediate story about a girl seeking asylum from an abusive stepfather dominated the news for a week. In the process of telling Christine's story, Todd and her fellow charitable ladies cast doubt on the police chief, who had seemed so supportive of Christine's attempt to run away from home at first. The ladies also implied that Dr. Mary Latham and the members of the Catholic Ladies' Benevolent Society cared more about what the stepfather wanted than they did for Christine.

Christine's case helped usher in a new phase for the home. Todd and the managers had been working to focus their charity and to learn the skills that operating a charity required. The new phase was about settling in. They now had a home that would be for children, and they were learning how to manage it. The next few months would be more about figuring out how to finance their charity than trying to define it.

8
GROWING PAINS

While the ladies were hammering out the details of their charitable activities, they made one very sound decision that gave the organization stability. They incorporated as the Ladies' Benevolent Society, first in 1888, and then again in 1896—which made the society a legal entity, separate from the ladies who served as its board of directors and separate from the employees of the home.

Throughout the 1890s, the home and the ladies who managed it were on a track toward success. They would even reach a point where their finances were secure and they enjoyed the respect of the community. But they were still learning the best way to manage their charity, and they made some questionable decisions. Sometimes they simply did not see far enough beyond the prejudices of the day.

In the year after Todd and her associates had dedicated their home to children, their charity appeared in the newspapers less frequently. For one thing, the children they were taking into the home had stories that were less dramatic than Christine's. To be sure, the children needed help; for example, one boy who stayed in the home that year had a brother who was working full time to pay the younger boy's expenses. These children's stories were considered less compelling, however.

Moving on from the fiasco of the failed hospital, and finally having fixed the well, Todd and her friends were happy to get the home into a daily rhythm of taking care of children. It was enough for them to focus on managing and keeping the home supplied. Moreover, they might have

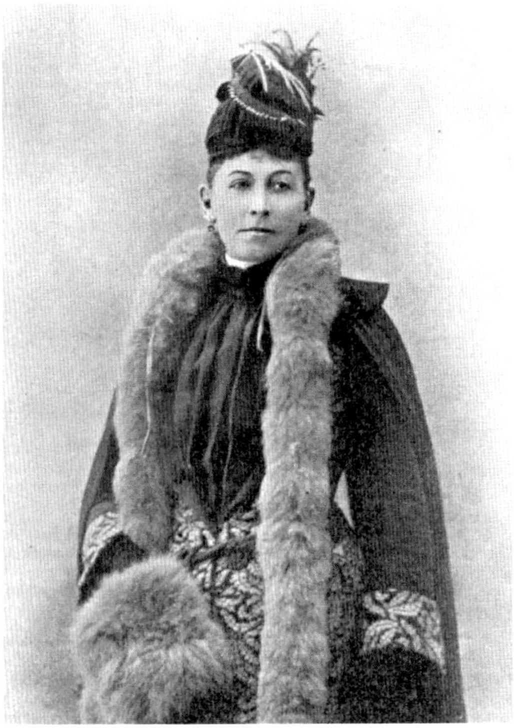

Alice Ide Houghton was active in women's clubs and sold real estate in the early 1890s. *Courtesy of the* Spokane Illustrated Supplement, *1890.*

been relieved to get out of the public eye for some time while they finalized the structure of their charity. Besides, Todd and her associates were doing what they said they would do. They were establishing a home. As long as it was working, there seemed little reason for reporters to check with the ladies. Many donors forgot about them too.

During the home's first six months, the ladies incurred $700 in debt. In an effort to get help, a group of ladies visited the city council again. They told the council members that they might have to close the home. In addition to asking the city leaders to pay their debt, the ladies requested that they budget $100 per month for the home. Council members listened to the ladies' request and promised to investigate some of the cases they discussed. The councilmen sent the financial request to their finance committee.

The next day, the ladies visited with the city finance committee. Alice Houghton, a well-known real estate agent, expressed the ladies' frustrations. She declared that a constitution forbidding the city to make charitable contributions should be banished.

After the ladies left, the city leaders discussed what they had heard. Two committee members thought they should put the matter off until a more expedient time; the third argued that the debt should be relieved immediately. They finally agreed to consider paying it, but since Spokane's charter did not allow the city to make charitable contributions, they chose not to make any further appropriations.

A month later, they still had not funded the debt, and instead of taking cash out of the city coffers to pay it, they discussed pulling about $4,000 from the 1889 Fire Relief Fund, which had been saved in a bank account. They passed a resolution in favor of the home, but opponents of the measure immediately asked that the resolution be reconsidered.

The city council eventually worked out a way to fund the Home of the Friendless monthly; so did the county. They also asked the managers to submit bills for services rendered. The rest of their funding came from individual donations and charity balls. By 1894, the ladies were keeping an average of forty children in the home each month. They had gotten past the earliest growing pains, and the home was an established charity.

9

DEFENDING THE HOME

Mary Todd served one year as president of the Ladies' Benevolent Society. She maintained a high profile, however, as a member of the society until after the home had been opened. She was still active enough in 1896 that she sat on a committee that reincorporated the home under revised Washington law. By that time, the president of the group was Lucy A. Ide, an aunt of Alice Houghton and one of the earliest white settlers of Spokane, who had traveled from Wisconsin in a wagon in 1878.

Despite facing some tight budget years, the Home of the Friendless was gaining stability. Ide and her associates discussed how to raise the money they needed. They managed the budget, oversaw the matron of the home, planned parties for the children and held balls or hops as often as twice a year to raise money. Moreover, they represented the home at city council and county commissioners' meetings and made sure that the charity had a full complement of employees, including a nurse and a cook. At Christmastime, they kept track of donated Christmas gifts and published a long list of the donors and their gifts in the newspaper.

As early as 1892, the Benevolent Ladies were averaging between thirty and forty children in the home per month. At the time, the charity had less than half the number of children that were housed in St. Joseph's Orphanage. The difference, according to city council members, who temporarily cut off appropriation to St. Joseph's that year, was that the Catholic orphanage took in children from across the region, whereas the home took in only children from Spokane.

In February 1897, shortly before Lucy Ide became president, the Ladies' Benevolent Society came very close to making Spokane lose faith in the home. An unannounced committee representing both the county commissioners and the city council visited St. Joseph's Orphanage and the Home of the Friendless to investigate conditions in both institutions.

The nuns at St. Joseph's supervised children and managed the orphanage, keeping all their records on-site. They could welcome an unexpected official delegation to come in and talk with the children, interview staff and look through their books. Their average occupancy, usually at least twice as large as that of the home, also impressed the committee.

On the other hand, Lucy Ide and her associates were managers. They spent most of their time away from their charity. They hired a matron, nurses and cooks and paid them to stay at the home with the children. Moreover, they kept neither their treasurer's records nor the secretaries' minutes of board meetings on site. Thus, when the delegation unexpectedly knocked on the door, the person who answered could talk about the children's activities or address their overall health, but she would not be able to give them a managerial perspective—nor would she necessarily know financial details. In fact, what the investigators found at the home was an itemized list of non-cash gifts. It listed things like a load of wood, a sack of potatoes, apples, toys and books—goods that had been donated whose worth the ladies had not quantified.

Ide was incensed to read in the February 3 issue of the *Spokesman-Review* that the investigative committee had suggested that the city and county unite to build a home for orphans.[6] The committee explained that the present institutions, to each of which the city was paying seventy-five dollars monthly, were insufficient to handle the number of children who were applying for admittance, including several children who had been turned away in the past month.

Ide called a meeting of the Board of Lady Managers for the next day. The "hopping mad" ladies met at Ide's home and held an "indignation meeting." Forgoing the customary pleasantries that preceded most meetings, the ladies began discussing their grievances immediately upon being called to order. They questioned the veracity of the committee, arguing that it was not representative of the "two honorable bodies" that the Board of Lady Managers had been working with for more than ten years.[7]

They resolved that the report was untrue and urgently requested that the city and the county appoint, from among their own members, someone who would take the time to make a proper investigation—one that would include examining the treasurer's reports and the secretaries' minutes of the meetings.

Shortly thereafter, Lucy Ide put the ladies' frustrations into a lengthy statement she sent to the *Spokesman-Review*. She carefully explained that they kept track of the type of gifts donated and published a yearly list of the donors' names, along with what they had donated. She noted that because many were small gifts—a sack of potatoes or a load of firewood—the ladies had chosen not to itemize the value of the gift. She went on to state that the home was owned and controlled by the Ladies' Benevolent Society, a legally incorporated body, and she defended its officers by name. Then she asserted that it would have been far more helpful for the investigators to ask to look at the treasurer's books to see how they spent the money that the city and the county gave the home each month.

She further claimed that the charity could house many more children, as many as seventy-five. Then she declared that Spokane should be proud of the home since it was "the only institution in eastern Washington that is conducted without respect to color, party, sect or creed."

The city council member who had visited the home agreed with Ide that the treasurer's books were probably in order. He countered, however, that the society probably received more than half of its sustaining donations in goods and produce. Because of this situation, he argued, the records the matron had showed him gave him sufficient information that he did not need to ask what the ladies did with the seventy-five dollars the city gave them each month. Although he did not go on, he could have made the case from his position that the home did not have sufficient resources to house as many as 120 children.

However, he did not seem to notice that the problem he observed might be better addressed by asking the city and the county to raise the subsidies paid to the orphanages. No doubt his suggestion that the city and county band together to establish a new orphanage would have cost the two government bodies more than simply raising their current subsidies would have. But this point was not discussed.

Ide and the Benevolent Ladies would have had to agree with his assertion that the home did not have sufficient resources to house seventy-five more children. But they were still indignant and looking for city leaders to make amends. So, after reading in the newspaper that he was deferring to the council on the matter, they quickly sent a copy of their resolution to Mayor H.N. Belt.

The ladies were especially disappointed in Belt, a political outsider who had won the mayor's office in 1894 and had spent much of his time advocating for reform. In the case of the home, however, his silence implied that the city council was correct. By sending him a copy of their resolutions, the ladies pushed him into saying more.

Belt responded, on February 10, by forwarding the resolutions to the city council and adding his own cover letter. Expressing his confidence that the council would be just, he suggested that they look for a way to establish an official report system that all similar institutions could use. He concluded by reminding them that the Benevolent Ladies were making a considerable personal sacrifice on behalf of the home.

The mayor's lukewarm response left the door open for further criticism of the home. On the next day, a letter, signed an "Orphan's Friend," appeared in the newspaper. It was from a reader who claimed not to be acquainted with the matron, asking whether a widespread rumor claiming that she had recently sent one of the children to school without any breakfast was true.

The society's president declared that there was no foundation for this question. The matron responded by claiming that it was not her policy, nor that of the home, to deny children their food as punishment. When a reporter pressed her further, she repeated her policy again. Finally, she admitted that it had happened once but added that she had decided it was not a good thing to do again. The lady managers and the matron accused the person who had written the anonymous letter of aiming to harm the home's reputation.

A week later, two weeks after the original complaints were published, someone on the city council—perhaps for the first time—read the ladies' list of indignations and decided that it made the investigating committee look bad. Accordingly, they invited the lady managers to come meet with them again.

On February 16, Ide and her associates attended a council meeting where they listened as Mayor Belt's letter and their list of resolutions were read. They followed up with a discussion about how the committee might be able to read their official treasurer's records and secretaries' minutes. The ladies still asked for the investigation that their resolutions had demanded.

The ladies were at first frustrated and then amazed and relieved upon hearing the responses. Councilman Dunning, a member of the investigating committee, said he hadn't changed his mind. Councilman Thompson, the most vocal member of the committee, who had told reporters two weeks earlier that the ladies' resolutions had not changed his position, had a change of heart. He stood up and said he thought the investigation that they had started should be finished, and he added that Dunning's position made him look unwilling to do more. The third councilman, Schiller, took an even more serious stand. He said that the ladies' resolutions made the investigating committee look bad and that the council's unwillingness to extend the investigation further would hurt their reputation. The vote was two to one. The ladies got their wish.

The lady managers were thrilled with the headline in the *Spokesman-Review* the next day, which read, "The Home Scores Once."[8] They told reporters that they were sure the extended investigation would prove the merit of their position. A prominent member of the society said that evening that the outcome was no more than she had expected. She further predicted that the new evidence they found would force the committee to announce that the home was well run.

Ide and her associates had been challenged by the controversy. Having city and county representatives—the very organizations that were paying most of their bills—publicly criticize their charity created problems. At times, they wondered whether the home would survive another decade. But just as they had made it through the early challenges of building, such as digging the well deep enough and establishing the best format for their charitable institution, they weathered a nationwide economic depression in the early 1890s and went through the storm of public criticism in the late 1890s.

The ladies came out of that controversy thinking about what they would need to do to help their home survive into the twentieth century. They would improve their system of reporting to the city and the county. During the new decade, they planned to create a much more stable reputation in the community. They did not always provide the unbiased charitable care they envisioned themselves providing, but the new decade would be a time of growth and financial stability.

10
A DAY AT THE HOME

Mattie B. Shaw, a veteran in women's work from Tacoma, Washington, woke up with the first light of dawn. Shaw was the new matron at Spokane's Home of the Friendless, and she wanted to get up before the thirty children awoke. She quickly slipped into her dress before grabbing the oil lamp near her bed and hurrying down to the second floor, where the youngest children slept.

The babies, one less than a year old and five aged up to three, would need help getting up and getting dressed. Morning was Shaw's favorite part of the day. Forty-three years old, she had been married for sixteen of those years but had not been able to have any children of her own. Helping these little ones get ready for their day eased some of the lump that grew in her throat when she thought about the children she had hoped for.

Ruth, the fourteen-year-old resident, would be by her side soon to assist. The teenager had been in the home for several years and had learned to help the matrons as they went about their day. Ruth could dress the little ones, escort the older children to school on time each day and usher them back to the home again in the afternoon.

As she worked with the little ones, Mattie could hear Sophia, the cook, bustling about in the kitchen preparing the morning's porridge. The benevolent ladies stressed making sure the children were fed sufficiently, and Sophia, the mother of seven surviving children, was well suited for this job. She could easily pull together meals for the forty or more people who ate at her tables each day.

While Mattie buttoned a three-year-old's dress, Ruth went next door to the older girls' room. She stood up to her full height and whistled loudly. Sleepy girls tumbled out of bed and began pulling dresses over their heads and tidying their hair. When Mattie finally made it into the room with the baby on her hip, the girls were making their beds.

Across the hall in the boys' room, Carl and Claude, eleven-year-olds, were making sure all the younger boys were awake. The boys who tried to stay in bed longer got an ear tweak or a thump on the chest. Mattie soon followed behind, checking each child to make sure he was well enough to attend school. One boy, nine-year-old James, said he had a sore throat, so Mattie sent him to talk to Nurse Jane.

At sixty-two years old, Nurse Jane was the senior member of the staff. She had few medicines and disapproved of giving kids sugar lumps soaked in brandy, but she pulled some chamomile tea out of her drawer, added a drop of honey to it and gave it to James. After she had coaxed him to drink all the tea, she sent him downstairs to join the others at the big dining room table.

As Mattie watched the children eat, she carefully made a mental list of the announcements she needed to make. One of the boys had lost a cap, and some girls had misplaced three hair ribbons. She would have another load of firewood to be stacked after school and wanted Carl and Claude to oversee the process. Finally, after school the next day, the lady managers would be coming to the home to oversee a harvest-themed party for all the residents. This afternoon the children would have to prepare their rooms for the visiting ladies, so it would be important for all the children to come straight home after school.

After each child had finished a bowl of porridge, all the children rinsed their dishes, put them in cloth bags and hung them to dry on a line stretching from one corner of the dining hall to the other. Then the oldest children helped the younger ones line up, and they all followed the oldest children through the arched doorway, heading to school.

Ruth helped the children aged four through six to line up. She would see them safely to kindergarten before going back to the home to help Sophia prepare the evening meal. She had completed elementary school the previous year, so she no longer went to school.

After the toddlers had enjoyed some playtime, Mattie settled the youngest down for their morning naps; then she helped Louisa carry the day's laundry out to the clothesline. With many of the children on their way to school, Mattie was free to prepare a report for Lucy Ide, president of the Ladies' Benevolent Society. The society president would be at the home around 2:00

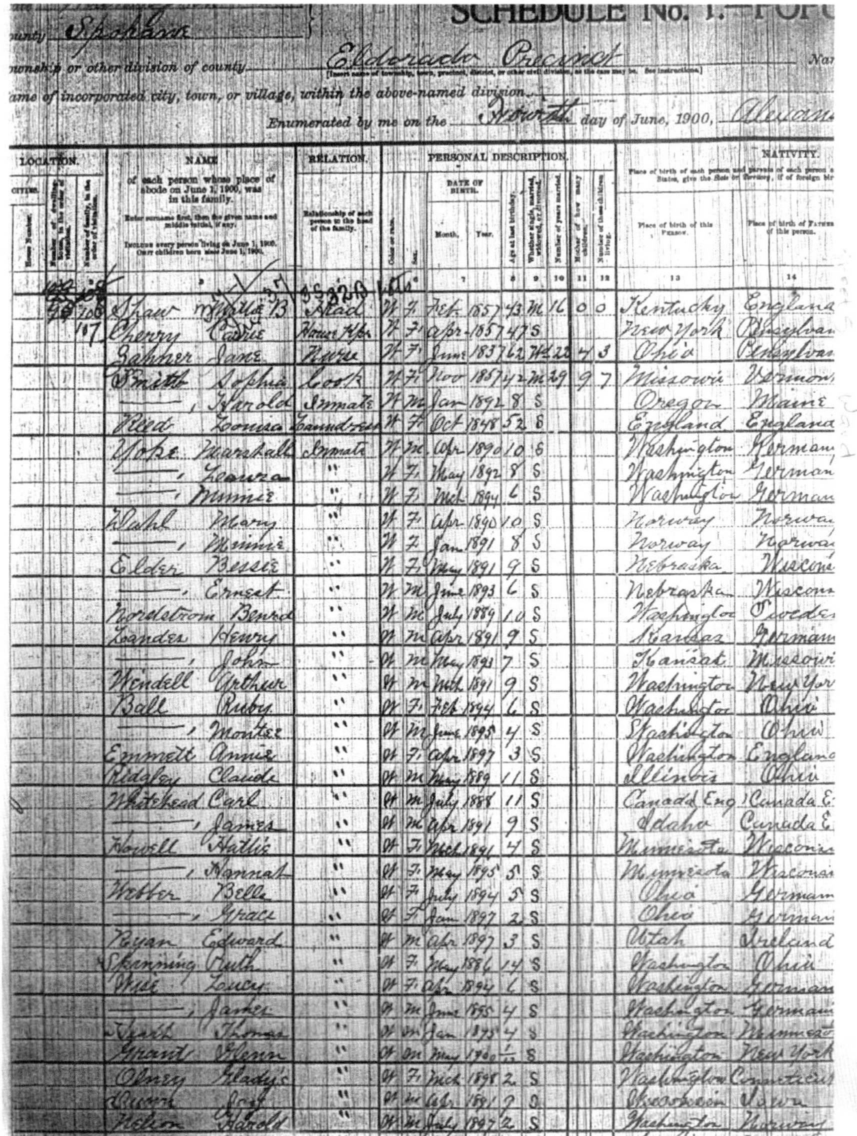

SCHEDULE No. 1.—POPU[LATION]

County: Spokane

Township or other division of county: Eldorado Precinct

Name of incorporated city, town, or village, within the above-named division:

Enumerated by me on the Fourth day of June, 1900,

Name	Relation	Color	Sex	Month	Year	Age	Marital	Years married	Mother of	Living	Place of birth	Father's birthplace
Shaw, [illegible]	Head	W	F	Feb	1857	43	M	16	0	0	Kentucky	England
Cherry, Carrie	House Kpr	W	F	Apr	1857	47	S				New York	Pennsylvania
Gahner, Jane	Nurse	W	F	June	1837	62	Wd	22	4	3	Ohio	Pennsylvania
Smith, Sophia	Cook	W	F	Nov	1857	42	M	29	9	7	Missouri	Vermont
—, Harold	Inmate	W	M	Jan	1892	8	S				Oregon	Maine
Reed, Louisa	Laundress	W	F	Oct	1848	52	S				England	England
Yoke, Marshall	Inmate	W	M	Apr	1890	10	S				Washington	Germany
—, Leaura	"	W	F	May	1892	8	S				Washington	German
—, Minnie	"	W	F	Mch	1894	6	S				Washington	German
Dahl, Mary	"	W	F	Apr	1890	10	S				Norway	Norway
—, Minnie	"	W	F	Jan	1891	8	S				Norway	Norway
Elder, Bessie	"	W	F	May	1891	9	S				Nebraska	Wisconsin
—, Ernest	"	W	M	June	1893	6	S				Nebraska	Wisconsin
Nordstrom, Bernard	"	W	M	July	1889	10	S				Washington	Sweden
Lander, Henry	"	W	M	Apr	1891	9	S				Kansas	German
—, John	"	W	M	May	1893	7	S				Kansas	Missouri
Wendell, Arthur	"	W	M	Mch	1891	9	S				Washington	New York
Ball, Ruby	"	W	F	Feb	1894	6	S				Washington	Ohio
—, Montee	"	W	M	June	1895	4	S				Washington	Ohio
Emmett, Annie	"	W	F	Apr	1897	3	S				Washington	England
Ridgley, Claude	"	W	M	May	1889	11	S				Illinois	Ohio
Whitehead, Carl	"	W	M	July	1888	11	S				Canada Eng	Canada E.
—, James	"	W	M	Apr	1891	9	S				Idaho	Canada E.
Howell, Hattie	"	W	F	Mch	[illegible]	4	S				Minnesota	Wisconsin
—, Hannah	"	W	F	May	1895	5	S				Minnesota	Wisconsin
Webber, Belle	"	W	F	July	1894	5	S				Ohio	German
—, Grace	"	W	F	Jan	1897	2	S				Ohio	German
Ryan, Edward	"	W	M	Apr	1897	3	S				Utah	Ireland
[illegible], Ruth	"	W	F	May	1886	14	S				Washington	Ohio
Wise, Lucy	"	W	F	Apr	1894	6	S				Washington	German
—, James	"	W	M	June	1895	4	S				Washington	German
[illegible], Thomas	"	W	M	Jan	1895	4	S				Washington	Minnesota
Grant, Glenn	"	W	M	May	1900	[illegible]	S				Washington	New York
Olney, Gladys	"	W	F	Mch	1898	2	S				Washington	Connecticut
[illegible]	"	W	M	[illegible]	[illegible]	[illegible]	S				Wisconsin	Iowa
Nelson, Harold	"	W	M	July	1897	2	S				Washington	Norway

A page from the 1900 census, listing the occupants of the Home of the Friendless. *U.S. Census, 1900.*

p.m. to review the report, shortly before the Benevolent Ladies would arrive to hold their semi-monthly meeting. The ladies met in the parlor twice a month, and Mattie made a mental note to have a pot of tea ready for the ladies to drink as they met.

After the babies woke up from their nap, Mattie changed their diapers and got them ready for lunch. Then she carefully walked them downstairs to the playroom, where they waited while Sophia set out a cold lunch of biscuits, jam and milk. While she gave the baby his bottle, Mattie thought about the story Mary Todd liked to tell, about finding babies in early Spokane who were starved for milk.

Once the baby had fallen asleep, Mattie put him in his crib and began preparing for the meeting of the Ladies' Benevolent Society. First, she needed to check with Nurse Jane and get the number of children who had been sick during the week. They had been passing colds around the home, but she thought they were mostly over them now.

As she climbed the stairs to the nurses' room, Mattie met Carrie, the housekeeper, sloshing a mop bucket on her way down the stairs. The housekeeper liked to mop the dormitory rooms' floors while the kids were away at school, and she always tried to dust the parlor so it would be ready for the Benevolent Ladies when they came for meetings. Mattie, understanding her haste, nodded as they passed.

Nurse Jane thought the colds were nearly gone, except for that of James, the one who had awakened with a sore throat that morning. She had given him some tea and hoped he would be on the mend soon. Just to make sure, she would ask him to sleep in the hospital room that night, away from the other kids.

While talking with the nurse, Mattie heard the front door open and saw Lucy Ide walk in. She smiled; this big-hearted lady was a dear to work for, and she loved the children as much as Mattie did. She would often bring a few apples along when she visited the home, just to give the toddlers a special treat for their lunch, or a couple of hair ribbons for the girls. And if the children tried hard enough, Ide would tell them a story about her wagon trip from Wisconsin to Spokane; the children would gather around to listen.

Mattie walked downstairs to meet Mrs. Ide, who on this occasion had brought some huckleberry preserves. Mattie greeted her warmly and thanked her for the gift. The children would have a special treat for the upcoming holidays.

Mattie reported to Lucy Ide that they had thirty-one children in the home, including one infant, who was doing fine. James, the nine-year-old, was the only one who currently had a sore throat, but Nurse Jane said the tea that one of the ladies had donated the previous week was taking care of it. The three boys and two girls who had been fighting colds the week before were all getting well. Mattie was also happy to report that the children were looking forward to the party the ladies were planning.

Mattie enjoyed her job and, for the most part, got along with the staff, the children and the Board of Lady Managers. She knew they appreciated her talents. In fact, she would soon request a raise, and the board would vote unanimously to give it to her. But Mattie B. Shaw was not the perfect matron, and there were limits to her patience.

11

CHARITABLE LIMITS

One morning in April 1900, Mattie Shaw opened the home's door to find an assistant to the Spokane county commissioners standing there. Beside him stood a small, sickly looking boy named Denny and Miko, a girl of Japanese descent. The county employee explained that these children were part of "Aunty Rogers's" family. And they needed a place to stay.

Mattie knew who Celia Rogers was. Everybody in Spokane knew of the flamboyant laundress who sang hallelujah hymns while standing beside a tub topped with overflowing bubbles at Spokane's annual Fruit Fair. She knew that when this former slave was not selling soap or doing laundry, she was tending to the needy children whom she had brought into her home.

Mattie understood that the laundress had little to call her own. She had seen Celia and her husband, Jimmy Rogers, with a family of miscellaneous children loaded into Jimmy's wagon. Recently, Rogers had been taking in more children than she could handle. Thus, she had started dropping infants off at the home or at St. Joseph's Orphanage.

Looking at the delegation at the door, Mattie assumed that Rogers was no longer able to care for any of her children. She listened as the assistant explained that Jimmy had been sick and had been admitted to the Spokane County Poor Farm, where he could get regular meals and better care. With Jimmy gone, the man explained, Celia did not have enough to feed the children. That is when the county had intervened.

Shaw took the children in, much as the home had done in the past. But this time, Denny was really sick. Unwilling to expose the other children to his illness, Shaw put him to bed in the hospital room.

The children would soon be home from school, so she left Denny with Nurse Jane and hurried back downstairs. Finding Miko shyly sitting in the entryway, she took the child's hand and led her to the girls' dormitory room, assigning her to a bed. Then she invited the girl to come with her as she hurried back downstairs. As they arrived at the door, they heard Ruth encouraging six-year-old Ernest to wait his turn and watched as she held the big front door open for the elementary-aged children to enter.

Shaw hurried to greet them. It was important for her to oversee their homecoming so that she could make sure they hung their coats on hooks and took their books upstairs to place under their beds. Then there were chores the children could do while they waited for the dinner bell.

The evening progressed smoothly. Dinner involved only minor infractions, like when four-year-old Hattie spilled her soup and nine-year-old Henry talked too loudly. Little Miko sat quietly and ate quickly. After dinner, Mattie sat with the children; she listened to their stories about school and read to them from the big Bible they kept in the dining room. Then it was time for everyone to have a quiet time, during which the children took care of their belongings and got ready for bed.

Just as they had begun, there was a knock on the door. Louisa opened it, and Mattie heard loud talking as she walked toward the entry. She arrived there in time to see Celia Rogers brush past her and head for the stairs. She was wearing a threadbare shawl, and she carried a corncob doll for Miko and a worn blanket for little Denny. Mattie resented the intrusion just before bedtime but said nothing because she knew the child would be happy to see Aunty Rogers.

She watched the big-hearted laundress make a beeline to the second-floor dormitory room for girls, where she found Miko sitting quietly on her bed. The child's smile lit up as she recognized her adopted mother and happily took the doll. Shaw watched as she helped some of the younger girls undress; the two sat and chatted, laughing occasionally in a way that filled the room and echoed out into the hallways.

The two went upstairs together to check on Denny in the infirmary. He was resting fitfully but stirred and smiled sleepily when Celia gave him his blanket. He was still feeing poorly, but the laundress was good at bringing out smiles, and this time was no exception.

Mattie interrupted about that time and quietly told Mrs. Rogers it was time for parents to leave and time for Miko to join the other girls in their room. She stood and watched while Rogers and the girl shared one more laugh, and then the three went downstairs. After Rogers had tucked the girl into bed, Mattie quietly escorted the laundress down the stairs and locked the door behind her.

While reporting the next morning, Nurse Jane seconded Mattie's suspicions. They both thought that Denny Rogers had been given opiates as a medication. They further agreed that his condition seemed to be getting worse. He was running a fever, his breathing was labored, his neck was swollen and his nose wouldn't stop running. Mattie decided that they should ask the doctor to check on him.

The doctor advised the women to give Denny more space, so Nurse Jane put him in a bed at the back of the room. The rest of the kids were well enough that there were no other children near him. Then Nurse Jane settled into a day of quietly tending to the boy.

Mattie saw Ruth and the other children off to school. With relief, she noticed that Miko even had a small smile on her face as she headed to school with the others. But the matron had a nagging worry in the back of her head about Denny.

The worry stayed with her throughout the day. She genuinely enjoyed the children in the home and did not like to see one die. Besides, losing one would not be good publicity for the charity. She and the Board of Lady Managers worked hard to keep the home and its children looking respectable.

That night, Celia Rogers visited again. She arrived during the group time and told the children some jokes. But she stayed on into quiet time, talking to Miko about her school day. Together, the two went up to the third floor and sang a song to Denny. Mattie again breathed a sigh of relief when she shut the door behind Rogers.

Mattie's new nightly routine included visits from Celia Rogers. She would come in the evening, laugh and talk with Miko and visit Denny. But the boy was getting weaker and weaker. Mattie and Jane decided, on the third day, to admit the boy to Sacred Heart Hospital.

During the night of the fifth day, little Denny died. Nurse Jane was sad. Mattie was thankful that the boy had died at the hospital, rather than at the home. She also hoped his death would allow the home to get back to a more normal schedule.

A week later, the Board of Lady Managers met. Mattie was quick to tell them that only Denny had died and no other children were sick. She also complained that noisy parents were persistently visiting the home and staying far too late.

Rogers's visits to the home did slow. After Jimmy Rogers came home from the poor farm, the couple managed to take Miko home. Celia did not need to visit anymore.

But Celia's troubles were not over. She was still getting more unwanted babies. Over the next twelve months, she took six more babies to the home.

In the spring of 1901, Mattie's patience had worn thin. When a county representative knocked on the door with yet one more of Celia Rogers's babies, Mattie lost her temper. She raised her voice and complained that "the home had already taken in six of her babies." To make matters worse, she asserted, each of the babies had been given "some type of opiate." Besides, she explained, the home should be freed of the burden of having to take in "bastard" babies collected by "the Celia Rogers doorstep method."

Celia Rogers's story demonstrates the limits of the home. The ladies did not want to deal with children who did not come from respectable families. They further did not like Rogers's way of caring for her children. Aunty Rogers had the biggest heart for kids. She understood, in a way that Shaw did not, that every child deserves to be loved and cared for.

The final footnote to this story comes from July 1903, when both Celia and Jimmy Rogers died suddenly. Jimmy was in the bed without even a blanket over him. Celia collapsed on the street hours later, with two children in tow.

When the county commissioners tried to place the two children, either in the Home of the Friendless or at St. Joseph's Orphanage, both charities refused them. One institution was fighting a bout of the measles and could not take more children. The other had pertussis going around.

The Board of Lady Managers and their employees were not as unbiased or as free of religious entanglement as they liked to think they were. Neither were the managers as connected with the employees as they needed to be. In years to come, that disconnection between the board and the daily—or, to be more specific, nightly—activities at the home would prove especially dangerous for the children the ladies were trying to keep safe, and nearly disastrous for the home.[9]

Nevertheless, at the turn of the century, the Home of the Friendless was stable financially and the managers had worked out a system for it. They enjoyed the support of both the county and the city and, by 1909, had become the model for a well-managed orphanage in the community. We will leave them now, ensconced in their charitable activities, to go back and trace a different strand of women's activism in Spokane.

Part Two

SEEKING WOMEN'S RIGHTS

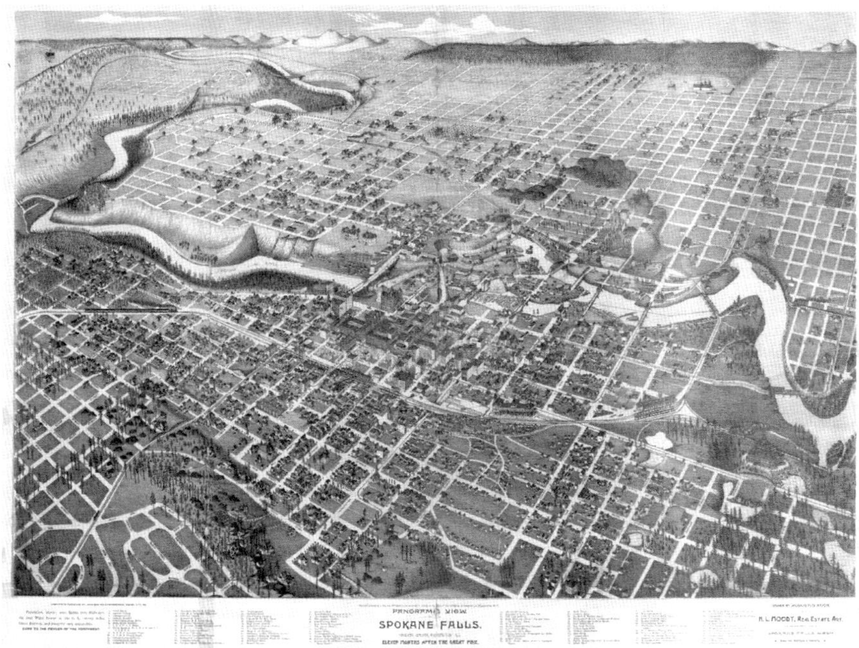

This 1905 map demonstrates how much the city changed in the preceding decades. *Courtesy of the National Archives.*

12

ROOTS OF WOMEN'S RIGHTS

If there was one organization that best represented the role of women in reform from 1870 through the turn of the twentieth century, it was the Woman's Christian Temperance Union (WCTU). Across the nation, more women were members of the WCTU than of any other women's organization. Spokane was no exception. The local WCTU was active well before the Ladies' Benevolent Society was organized.

Charlotte Pinkham Hamblen migrated to Spokane from Minnesota in 1887, along with her husband, father and four children. She was energetic, loved to chat with friends and enjoyed social activism, much as her father had taught her. She had an inquisitive mind and liked participating in organizations and charities.

Charlotte's activism and charitable involvement was a family affair. One afternoon, her teen daughters, Lizzy and Mabel, went around town asking florists to donate flowers that they could take to patients in the hospital. Charlotte's husband, Charlie, joined Chautauqua and attended meetings with her. Her father, Peter Coffin Pinkham, supported women's rights and helped keep the family informed about current events. Her son, Laurence, would grow up to become a prominent attorney in Spokane and represent a new generation of Lady Managers.

Charlotte and her family lived first on the near north side of the city. They could stand on their porch on North Monroe Street and watch the Spokane River go over the falls. The family was now established in their adopted hometown and would contribute to the city of Spokane for generations.

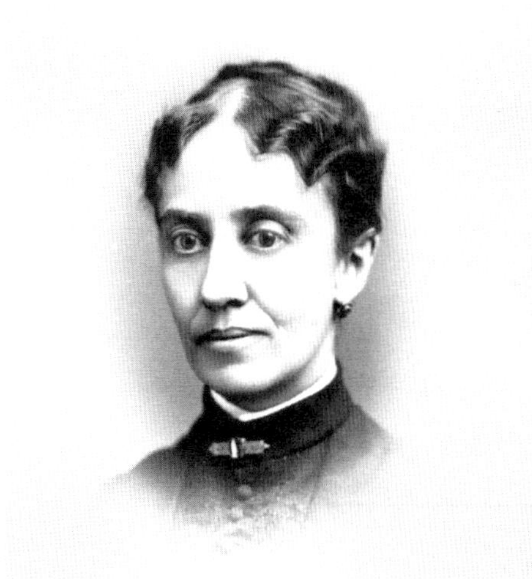

Right: Charlotte Pinkham Hamblen, late 1880s. *Courtesy of Anne Chamberlain.*

Below: The Hamblen family lived at Monroe and Broadway when they first moved to Spokane. *Courtesy of the Eastern Washington State Historical Society: Museum of Arts and Culture.*

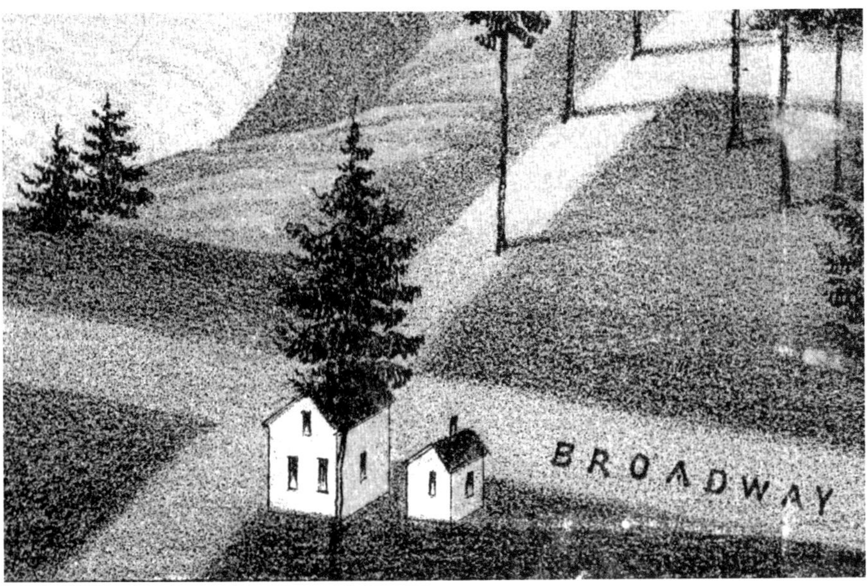

Soon after the Hamblen family moved to town, Charlotte met Angeline Crystal, founder of the Crystal Union, a local branch of the WCTU. Charlotte was accustomed to joining women's reform organizations, so she was delighted to find the Crystal Union and quickly became the treasurer. Charlotte and Angeline became best friends and worked together for the cause of temperance for the next two years. When the statewide WCTU meetings were held in 1888, Charlotte joined the group representing Spokane.

Charlotte also got acquainted with Mary Todd and Lucy Ide and learned about the Ladies' Benevolent Society. The ladies had been active before she moved to Spokane, but Charlotte was in town early enough that she joined Todd and several others in signing the society's Articles of Incorporation on April 4, 1888, and by doing so pledged to be a trustee of the corporation for the year. She would remain a leader in that charity through 1896, when state laws had changed sufficiently that the ladies decided to reincorporate.

In addition to helping the poor and promoting temperance, Charlotte supported women getting the vote. When she moved to Washington Territory, women had the right to vote. An 1883 ordinance had given them that privilege. Since then, a number of women had voted in local and state elections, and a handful had served on the city election board, even on a few juries. But in 1887, when Charlotte arrived, Spokane residents were participating in a statewide discussion about establishing Washington as the forty-second state. Part of that discussion was about whether the state would incorporate the right of women to vote into its new constitution.

Charlotte and her friends were irritated in early 1888 when a number of prominent businessmen in Spokane, its Board of Trade, began collecting more than two thousand signatures from people, especially women, who were opposed to including women's right to vote in the new constitution. The Benevolent Ladies did not agree with the business leaders, nor did they share the men's fear that giving women the vote would interfere with local mine owners' efforts to annex north Idaho's mining territory into the state of Washington.

The ladies further saw the irony in the Bloomer Case, which originated in Spokane. A prominent local attorney, George Turner, who was currently serving on the Territorial Supreme Court, helped behind the scenes while John Todd, a local bottler and saloon owner—as well as the husband of Mary Todd—devised a lawsuit that tied up the question of women's suffrage in the court system while Washington became a state. They arranged with Nevada Bloomer, who was a nominal suffragist at best, to vote in Todd's saloon. The election board, which John Todd sat on, threw her vote out. The resulting legal case, *Bloomer v. Todd et al*, tied up the question of a woman's right to vote while Washington Territory was establishing its constitution.[10]

Charlotte had long been interested in women's rights, and she was happy to be able to vote. She quickly met with Angeline Crystal and several other women to make plans to combat the local forces against women's right to vote. They decided to hold a mass meeting to talk about the issue. They secured a large hall and invited May C. Jones, the city's first woman pastor, to speak. They also invited an attorney and veteran of the Civil War, Colonel W.D. Turner, to speak. Finally, Charlotte and her friends went about town putting up posters and inviting people to attend their mass meeting.

The ladies thought the meeting was a grand success. May Jones, who was always polite and careful not to endorse controversial positions, gave a "pleasant and effective speech." Less concerned about offending people, Colonel Turner amused the audience by criticizing the editors of a local paper for saying that woman suffragists were "male women" and "cackling sisters." He also told his audience that the *Spokesman-Review* was a "puny paper," and then he lashed out at his own brother, attorney George Turner, who had written the anti-suffrage opinion on the Territorial Supreme Court's Harland decision. Crystal wrapped up the meeting, leading the audience as it selected a series of resolutions preserving women's right to vote.

The next morning, Charlotte complained in her diary that the editor of the *Spokesman-Review* had mocked their meeting, saying it had been sparsely attended. She was so upset about the article that she canceled her subscription to the paper and ordered the newsboy to get off her property.

Charlotte carried on with her usual busy life throughout the summer of 1889. There were WCTU meetings and Ladies' Benevolent Society events to attend. At the same time, she and Charlie were working on building a house on the south side of town. The summer passed quickly, and Charlotte was out of town when fire swept through six blocks of downtown Spokane.

The WCTU ladies of Spokane County sent a delegation of women to Olympia to observe as seventy-five men met there to draft a new constitution. The temperance ladies arranged with attorney Edward Eldridge, a delegate from Whatcom County, who was a former Speaker of the House and a five-time delegate, to propose striking the word "male" from the description of eligible voters.

The suffragist observers who had gathered in Walla Walla watched with great interest as Eldridge made his proposal. John Hoyt, a lukewarm suffragist himself who had been on the Supreme Court and had written the pro-suffrage opinion in the Harland Case, succumbed to the fear that Washington residents would vote down the state constitution if it included giving women the right to vote. What he did not explain was that he had agreed to limit suffragists' strength if he were given the job of chairman of the constitutional convention. Instead, he suggested making women's right to vote a separate article for Washington voters to decide upon, independent of the constitution issue. With lumps in their throats, the ladies watched the delegates vote Eldrige's proposal down, 50 to 8.

Washington State voters approved the constitution on October 1, 1889. They voted down the women's suffrage article, and Charlotte Hamblen would live the rest of her life without being able to vote. But that was still in the future.

Only two months after the referendum on the constitution, on the day that the family was moving into their new home, Charlotte's husband collapsed and died suddenly. Charlotte and her children managed to complete the move, but she was heartbroken. And she no longer found the drive to keep writing in her diary. She made occasional entries, noting, for example, the day on which she sent her son Laurence off to law school. But she would never again consistently record the daily comings and goings of her family.

Hamblen did, however, keep her family together. The children were educated, and Charlotte maintained the residence at City View on the South Hill for many more years. Because her son Laurence followed Charlotte's footsteps into civic activism, a sizeable section of the lower South Hill was developed eventually into Hamblen Park and Hamblen Elementary School.

13

THE WCTU AND EQUAL RIGHTS

Charlotte Pinkham Hamblen's support for voting rights for women merged with her interest in temperance. Members of the early Woman's Christian Temperance Union movement had been very careful to separate their interest in alcohol reform from advocating for voting rights. By the time Charlotte joined the group in Spokane, the organization had officially adopted the idea that women should seek to use the vote to gain more control over the abuse of alcohol.

Charlotte had noticed the five large brewery buildings when she first arrived in Spokane. They were so big she could see them from her home overlooking the falls. She observed that these "castles" were putting out beer by the bucket, both supplying pubs and sending out wagons loaded with filled buckets to leave on private doorsteps.

As Charlotte made friends with temperance ladies, she heard about their earlier attempts to clean up Spokane. In 1884, the WCTU formally appealed to city leaders to have voting places taken out of saloons. Saloon owners, who enjoyed a fair amount of business on voting days, interpreted the women's request as an attempt to hurt their business. They quickly began posting signs in their windows that said "What the WCTU wants we don't want."

By 1887, when Hamblen joined, the group was intent on changing the political situation in Spokane and on limiting alcohol's control over their city and its politics. They knew that the city had a large number of saloons per capita—as many as one per two hundred citizens—and they were looking for ways to limit alcohol's control.

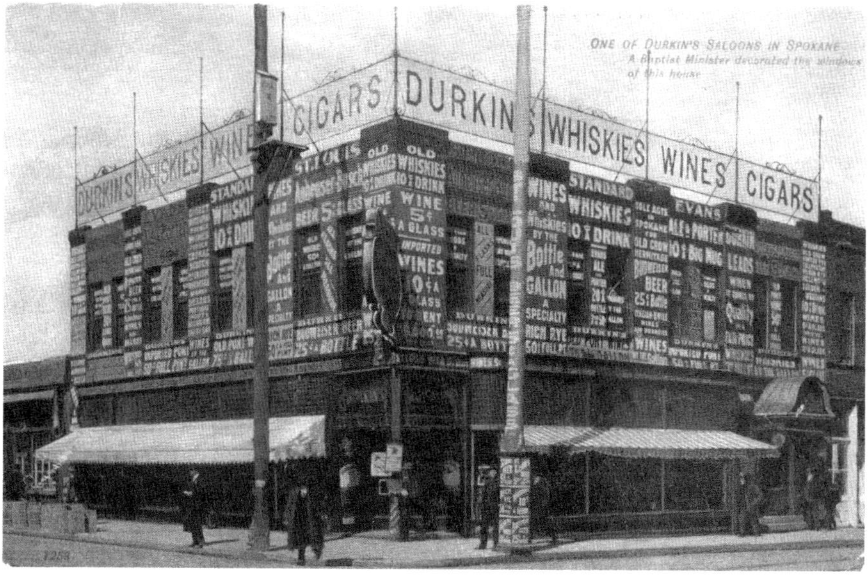

A large saloon owned by James Durkin in the 1880s. *Courtesy of the Eastern Washington State Historical Society: Museum of Arts and Culture.*

One of the people Charlotte got acquainted with was Lucy Switzer, wife of the druggist in Cheney. In October 1880, Switzer had organized the first union of the WCTU in Washington Territory, in Colfax. Only a few months later, she pioneered the suffrage movement in eastern Washington. As early as September 1881, she became the recording secretary of a group of suffragists who organized in Spokane. They met at a local church that had been founded by the Methodists a year earlier. The group signed a petition and resolved that they were looking for the "civil and political rights" that men now enjoyed to be given to "all naturalized citizens in the United States."[11] And in 1883, Switzer organized women in ten different towns in eastern Washington prior to the arrival of Frances E. Willard, national WCTU president, who formalized the eastern Washington WCTU in late July.

By the time Hamblen arrived in the area, the WCTU had been active for several years. Charlotte read eagerly in the *Union Signal* the articles that Switzer wrote about the eastern Washington WCTU and the national organization. By 1888, Charlotte had taken an important position in the Crystal Union, the WCTU group based on the north side of the river. In May of that year, she was elected delegate to the territorial convention scheduled for North Yakima the following spring.

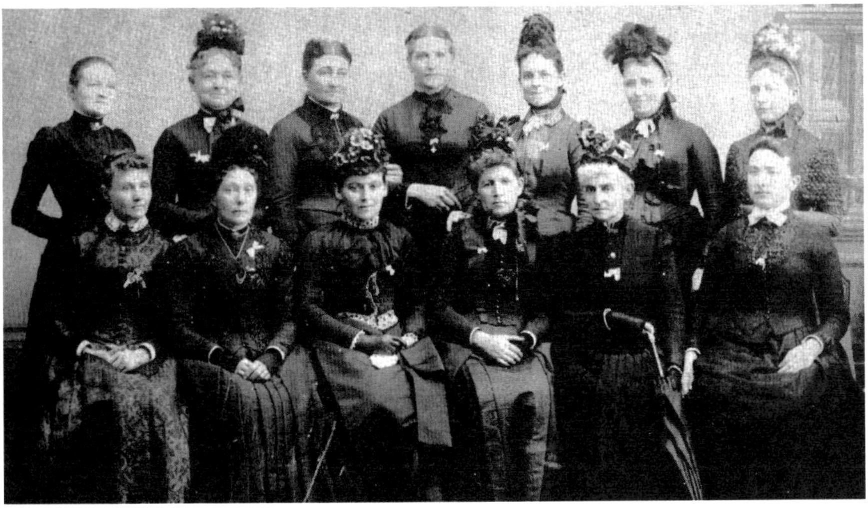

Eastern Washington WCTU members, including Lucy Switzer (*front row, fourth from left*) and Charlotte Pinkham Hamblen (*likely back row, far right*). *Courtesy of the Ned M. Barnes Northwest Room, Spokane Public Library.*

Besides attending regional meetings, Charlotte kept busy with the local WCTU. The Crystal Union met regularly on Wednesdays. When she was not in meetings, Charlotte was teaming up with other members to work on projects, help raise money and even entertain visitors from other unions and other regions. At a Ladies' Benevolent Society meeting in 1888, the management team excused Charlotte and a temperance friend because the two needed to go shopping for furniture to put in a new headquarters building.

The Crystal Union had recently moved into a building within walking distance of the Hamblens' home on the corner of Monroe and Broadway. It had three rooms upstairs, and Charlotte, her children and a few friends took on the responsibility for cleaning the building. Charlotte's teenage daughters, Mabel and Lizzy, and her son, Laurence, helped when they were not in school.

When Charlotte was not out visiting friends or attending meetings, she and her family entertained a steady stream of visitors and sometimes even enlisted their guests to help make candy or taffy for numerous socials or, occasionally, even to sell at nearby shops. That fall, Charlotte squeezed in time to help make a wedding cake and decorations for a temperance friend's wedding.

Already interested in winning for women the right to vote, Charlotte was happy to learn that the local WCTU had been active throughout the 1880s in advocating for women's right to vote. They had appealed to the city to take polling places out of saloons. Furthermore, they had seen to it that the city's polling places were equipped with large buckets of ice water as an alternative to providing beer for people coming in to vote.

Moving to Spokane in the late 1880s, Charlotte arrived there in time to participate in a discussion about women in the local jail. The temperance ladies were concerned because women who were arrested and put into jail were stuck in a seedy men's world for the duration of their stay. They were searched by men, and they were surrounded by male inmates and jailers while incarcerated.

For example, in 1887, a Seattle woman had been jailed in Spokane for grand larceny. The woman spent ten months sleeping in a hospital bed usually used for sick inmates, located in an open space between two cell wings. She had been supervised by men and had shared all her meals with the male convicts, and if she wanted to bathe, she had to do so in the same area where she slept.

Charlotte and the other WCTU members knew that there were women serving time in Spokane's jails. They believed that the women inmates should be treated differently than their male counterparts. They worried that female prisoners did not have sufficient blankets or clean clothes. And they disliked the idea of a woman who had been arrested having to be searched by men.

This concern, coupled with the WCTU's tradition of activism, led Charlotte and her friends to begin a quest to introduce women's wisdom, and their presence as helpers, into the local jails. These early requests were the first steps in what turned into a twenty-year endeavor to convince the city that it needed a police matron to supervise women who were doing time in jail.

Charlotte and her friends in Spokane knew they were not alone. In 1893, temperance activists had joined together in the state of Washington to get a law passed that required cities with populations of over ten thousand residents to hire a police matron to work in their local jails. Spokane's population, which was nearing twenty thousand by this time, was one of three cities in the state that the law applied to.

When news of the law reached Spokane, the local police and sheriff's departments dismissed it. Charlotte and her temperance friends were disappointed to hear the police argue that there was no room in their jails to give women a place to work. But they understood their position. Local institutions across the board were feeling the effect of the population boom that followed the 1889 fire in Spokane. Schools were filling up, the nuns at

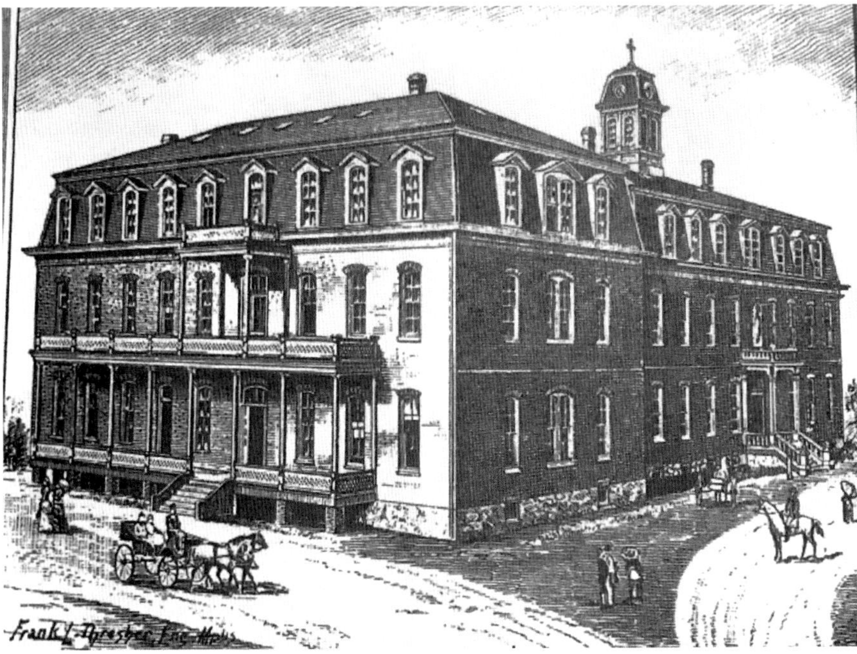

Sacred Heart Hospital with its first wing. *First published in Harry Hook and Francis McGuire,* Spokane Falls Illustrated, *Spokane Board of Trade, 1889.*

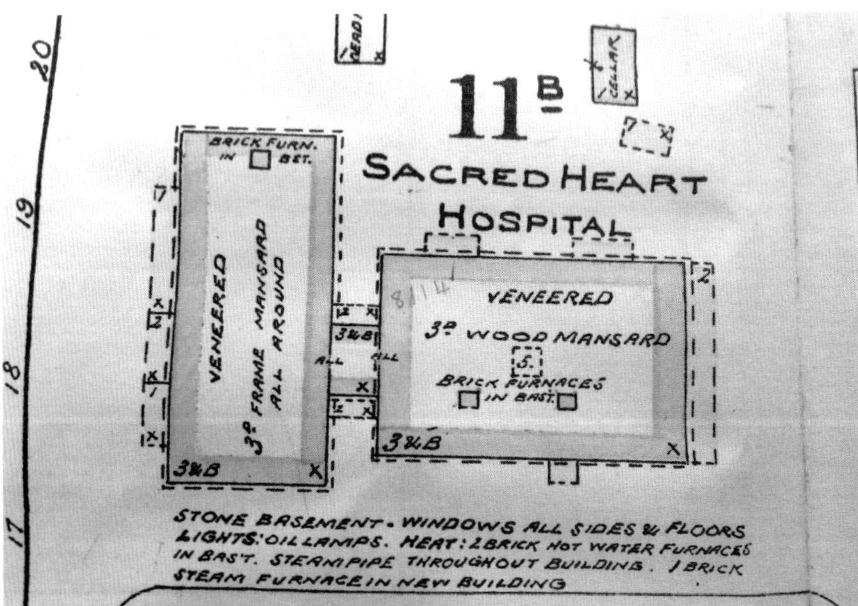

Imprint of Sacred Heart with its first wing, which Mother Joseph designed. *Courtesy of an 1890 Sanborn Map.*

Sacred Heart Hospital were making plans for a second addition to their hospital, the police department had doubled in size and the jails were overcrowded.

At the same time, by the middle of 1893, the nation was going through an economic depression, one that hit investors in Spokane especially hard. Many businesses had gone into debt to construct bigger and better buildings after the fire. Now, when the economic downturn came, the ladies saw businesses folding and genuine hardship in many areas around the city.

The poor economic conditions put a damper on their requests for a matron. It was hard to request a new building that would accommodate matrons. The economic conditions also dampened the ladies' efforts to give women the right to vote.

14
STRONG WOMEN

As the 1890s wore on, Spokane's WCTU members slowed down. The Crystal Union, on Spokane's north side, stopped meeting weekly and, within a year, had relinquished control of its headquarters rooms near Monroe Street. A.P. Crystal, the president and namesake of the union, moved away from the city. Charlotte Pinkham Hamblen had moved to the south side of town and was far less active than she had been in the 1880s.

By mid-decade, several of the WCTU unions had banded together into one larger Spokane Union. The temperance women still knew how to make formal requests of city leaders, however. For example, they would continue to address the need for police matrons. But Charlotte was never as active in the organization as she had been during her first years in Spokane.

A reform league, careful not to carry on the WCTU's wholesale objection to saloons or further their endorsement of suffrage, worked to do things like rid the city of "undesirable women" and attempt to close local businesses on Sundays. Women's clubs that were less activist in nature were becoming more popular. Many ladies joined literary groups. In these groups, designed by the women to educate themselves, members focused on doing research and presenting papers. For example, Harriet Ross established a group named the Twentieth Century Club. Ross and the other women took pride in their knowledgeable presentations, and they worked to impress Spokane leaders with their efficient management style. Alice Ide Houghton presided over the Sorosis Club, and its members pursued similar interests. Anna Stratton Browne, an active member in many women's clubs, helped oversee

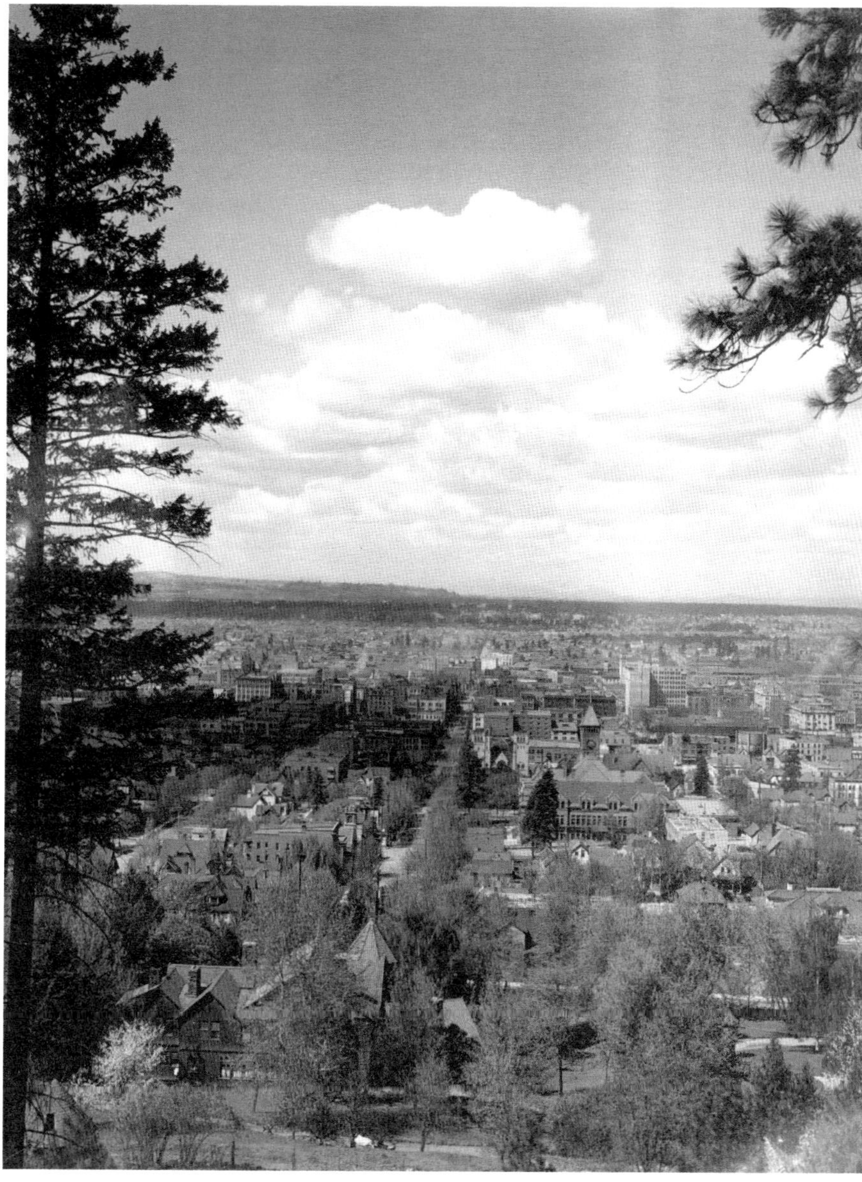

View of Spokane from the lower South Hill, 1908. *Courtesy of the Ned M. Barnes Northwest Room, Spokane Public Library.*

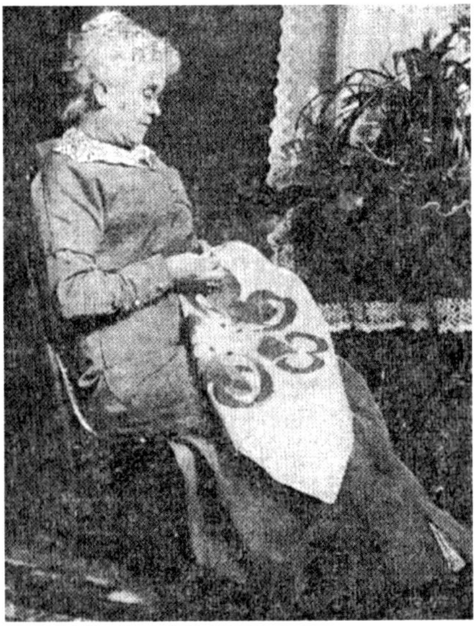

Harriet Ross (Gandy), twenty years after the fire. *Courtesy of the* Spokesman Review.

a reciprocity bureau through which Spokane women could enjoy the papers prepared by club women across the state, as well as share their own best work. Other groups focused on music, an arena in which skilled women could find an outlet for their talents.

In April 1898, Spokane's club women were abuzz with activity. The Washington State Federation of Women's Clubs planned to hold its annual meeting in Spokane that coming June. Ross and her friends, along with members of several other women's clubs, were thrilled. They wanted to showcase the city, to demonstrate to the rest of the women in Washington what a friendly and respectable city they lived in. They also were in charge of making local arrangements. This included securing affordable transportation to and from Spokane, as well as providing hospitality to the women who would be visiting their city. They announced they would be establishing a "bureau of information" that would keep train schedules and monitor the arriving mail. In addition, they would have reports about outside news, such as the latest events involving the Spanish-American War. The ladies also were planning a welcome reception for the group, to be held at the Hotel Spokane. Finally, they tried to arrange for a streetcar excursion that the delegates could enjoy.

Only ten days before the opening reception in the Hotel Spokane, the *Spokane Chronicle* published an article titled "Women Who Think."[12] It displayed the complete program for the meeting of the State Federation of Women's Clubs. The event, slated for the First Methodist Church, would begin on Tuesday, June 14, at 1:30 p.m. and end on Thursday, June 16, at 5:00 p.m. The meetings would begin with an invocation by the Reverend Rosine Edwards, pastor of the Congregational church located in nearby Hillyard. The event would feature presentations from the state officers and musical selections performed by women from Spokane. The delegates would enjoy reports from clubs all over the state along with presentations, such as the one on the statewide women's club movement, and Abigail Scott

Duniway, the well-known regional suffragist, presented "Greetings from Oregon." It would end on Thursday afternoon with a song by a chorus made up of Spokane ladies.

The convention began on time. The church, beautifully decorated by the Spokane Floral Association, was fragrant with fresh evergreen stems and flowers. Ross, Browne and other Spokane club women had worked diligently on the arrangements. They happily told reporters that the event was an example of the best qualities of Washington women. They explained that it demonstrated that they could be strong, refined and womanly and still could study to arouse their best ambitions. The *Chronicle* editor described them as "women of the nineteenth century who rule the West."[13]

15

ARE THE WOMEN ASLEEP?

Carrie Hill, a little lady from Seattle who attended the convention in Spokane, talked to a *Chronicle* reporter on June 15. Middle-aged, with graying hair at her temples, this president of Washington's Equal Suffrage Association quietly told the reporter how the women of Washington planned to campaign for the upcoming referendum on a constitutional amendment that would give women the right to vote.

They would, Hill said, organize a working club in each ward in the city. These clubs, in turn, were to knock on doors in their section of town to ask the residents whether they supported the proposed amendment and generally try to convince them to sign petitions supporting giving women the right to vote. In addition, the ward clubs were to call meetings to help educate their voters about suffrage. They might demonstrate, for example, how other states—such as Idaho, which had recently given women the right to vote—were experiencing the effect of women's suffrage for the first time. While visiting in the wards, the suffragists were to gather signatures on a petition that would be delivered to political caucuses meeting later in the season.

Hill went to on explain that agrarian voters—and conservatives who wanted to expand the money supply—were big supporters of the proposed amendment. She noted that in Washington State, the agrarians, known as populists, supported including the proposed suffrage amendment on the ballot. Beyond formal political parties, labor unions and WCTU members were also important supporters of suffrage in the state.

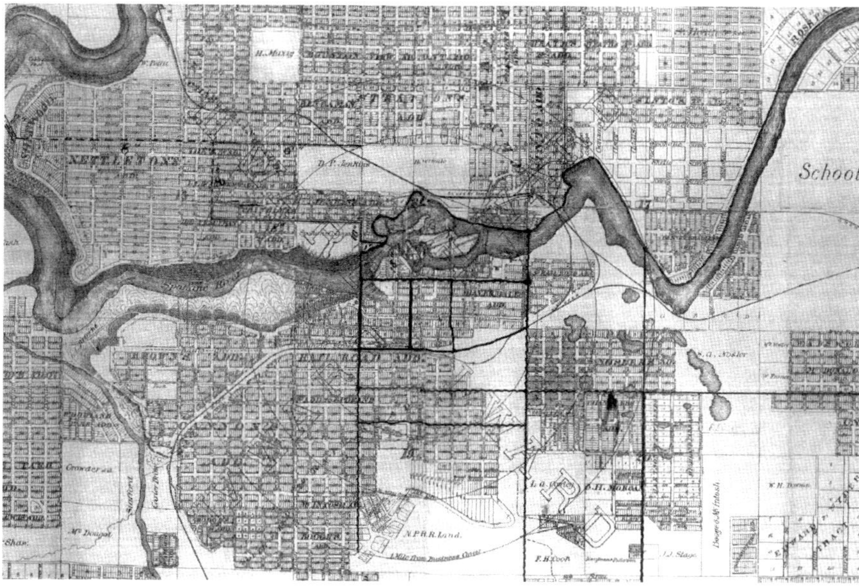

This 1889 map has the voter precincts outlined on it, with the first through fourth on the south bank of the river. *Spokane County Auditor, Precinct Map, Courtesy of Washington State Archives, Eastern Regional Branch.*

Two days later, Hill met with several women in Spokane to begin the process of establishing ward clubs. Among the ladies in attendance were Lida Ashenfelter—a widow and a longtime WCTU member—and Anna Stratton Browne. They were joined by a newcomer to Spokane's suffrage scene, Mrs. L.W. Hutton—May Arkwright Hutton—a future suffrage leader in the state who at that time still resided in Idaho. She had already legally voted and twice served on the local board of elections.

Since there wasn't enough time to organize each ward club, the group selected three women charged with coordinating the local suffrage drive. Two were WCTU members: Ashenfelter and Rose Winstead. The third member was to be Florence Kent, a local teacher and principal. The three ladies knew many women in Spokane and were active in numerous women's clubs.

Then, having selected a committee, the ladies lingered; almost loath to leave the meeting, they discussed a number of other ideas. They finally left with high hopes of helping to win the state for suffrage. But they were exhausted from just having hosted the convention for the State Federation of Women's Clubs. In addition, it was almost time for Spokane's residents to leave for their traditional summer break at a nearby lake.

On June 29, almost two weeks later, a *Chronicle* reporter encountered Florence Kent on the street. He asked her what had happened with the local suffrage movement since Hill had left. The committee had met, Kent told him, and they had decided that it would be better to wait to begin organizing in the wards until later in the season. Disappointed, the reporter asked if there would be no more suffrage work completed during the summer break. Florence explained that the committee members would be doing minor work in the meantime but would save most of the effort until later.

The Fourth of July came and went with the city's usual celebrations. Many Spokane residents found their way to nearby beaches and lake cabins for extended visits. The club women who remained in the city concentrated on establishing a Red Cross chapter so that they could more directly contribute to the war effort.

16

SEEKING SUFFRAGISTS

On August 26, eight weeks before the election, Carrie Hill returned to Spokane. She happily reported that the statewide suffrage movement was developing better than anyone had expected. There were eight organized ward clubs in Seattle, and the members were canvassing a large number of women there to find out who supported equal suffrage. When asked to clarify where the movement was successful, she replied, "All over the state—almost everywhere except in Spokane."[14]

Before she left the reporter's office, Hill described a list she had collated of able speakers who were voluntarily representing the cause at meetings across the state. She said that she hoped to have one of these speakers come to Spokane soon. In the meantime, she invited all of Spokane's suffragists and anti-suffragists alike to attend a meeting at the Christian church at eight o'clock that evening.

The meeting went well. Hill supervised as the women formed two ward clubs, and she began the process of collecting signatures for a suffrage petition. After the clubs were established, Hill instructed the members to go house-to-house canvassing for signatures in support of women's right to vote. She also asked them to distribute suffrage literature. Hill was very excited about the newest brochures she left with the members, because they actually contained information offered by ladies who lived in states that had already given women the right to vote.

Less than a week later, four of Spokane's five wards had suffrage clubs. The women leading each group were a mixture of longtime members and others new to the club scene. Mrs. L.H. Prather, wife of a prominent lawyer in town, was president of the first ward club. Well known among her peers, Edna was a natural to organize the first ward suffragists, and she had an assistant and two secretaries to help her.

Lillie Steeper, new to the club scene in Spokane, became president of the second ward club. She was excited about helping women get the right to vote and had already begun to canvass the ladies in her ward. She also was fortunate to have a longtime WCTU member, Francine M. Buck, to help her.

The third ward had Esther A. Jobes, an ardent suffragist, who helped manage a family-owned grocery store. When she was not promoting giving women the right to vote, she enjoyed participating in literary women's clubs. Jobes was happy to coordinate suffragists in her ward, but she was having difficulty finding anyone else to help her there.

In the fourth ward, four new clubwomen took the lead. They did not have a lot of experience, but they were excited about promoting the suffrage amendment in their neighborhoods. The four ladies were confident that they could complete their canvass of the ward in time.

Josephine Dunning took the presidency of the fifth ward club. A veteran club woman, she enjoyed patriotic, literary and charitable clubs. One of her helpers was Josephine Brinkerhoff, a longtime member of artistic and literary clubs. Two more women added willing hands to the committee. These volunteers were not so well connected among club women but were happy to help to campaign for women's voting rights.

The second ward club had the first canvass results. Only a week after she had been selected to head the ward club, Steeper announced that she had already found 27 women who supported suffrage, with only 1 opposed. A week later, the ward two canvass had identified 242 women for suffrage, 3 who didn't care and 6 who were opposed. The first ward found 118 suffragists and 3 opposed. The fourth and fifth wards did not have exact numbers, because they had handed out petitions that they were still waiting to have turned in. The third ward had not even found enough signers for the petitions, and thus, the ward could not pull together enough people to create a club.

On September 20, Steeper and the other suffragists collated the signatures they had collected and entrusted them to the care of a delegate heading to the Washington State Republican Convention. Suffragists from all over the state were doing the same thing.

The petitioners at the convention were asked to stand up at an appointed time and present the names of people from their county seeking approval for the suffrage amendment. The ladies planned that this would provide a number of people standing at the same time throughout the audience, which would present a visual image of a lot of people supporting the suffrage amendment.

Once the ward clubs had sent their petitions to the statewide conventions, the Spokane clubs lost momentum. Steeper had no more petitions to announce—neither did the leaders of the fourth and fifth ward clubs.

They at least squeezed in a few meetings. Steeper and the suffragists in ward two had a meeting in early October. But if they made any significant progress, they did not make a formal announcement about it.

17

"MEAN" TRICKS

In late fall of 1898, the suffrage battle switched from women knocking on doors in Spokane's wards to its postal service. Anti-suffragist literature arrived in Spokane in mid-October in the form of an article that had first appeared in a Boston paper. Then women living in New York who opposed suffrage republished it in pamphlets and put them in the mail.

The anti-suffragists knew Washington was considering an amendment to its constitution giving women the vote, so they began targeting the state with mail. The *Chronicle* editor dutifully read the material and summarized its message in the paper. The antis asserted that having the vote would damage women's influence. Although their example seemed weak, they argued that because temperance was so much more widely supported than suffrage, there was no need for temperance women to have the vote.

On the other hand, Mrs. Carrie Hill and her associates in Seattle were happily sending out pamphlets informing Washington voters about the experiences of states in which women had already been given the right to vote. That fall, they decided to dig out the state's own records of women voting during its territorial days. They began publishing what newspapers in Washington Territory had reported in 1884 when women briefly had full voting privileges. They sent this literature to suffrage clubs all over Washington.

In addition to making sure local editors received copies of the suffrage brochures, Steeper and her colleagues gave the materials to other key voters in the city. On October 17, the *Chronicle* published "Mean Trick by Suffragists."[15] The article praised the ladies, saying the idea to quote newspapers from 1884 demonstrated how smart and well informed they were.

The *Whatcom Reveille* had noticed that candidates for office were dressing better since women had become qualified voters. The *Dayton Chronicle* reported that the women who came to vote were treated respectfully. It added that women had voted their consciences and—although some admitted they had made mistakes—the paper believed the women had made fewer errors than their male counterparts. The *Sprague Herald* said that women added charm and prestige to the polling places.

Not to be outdone by the suffragists, Mrs. W. Winslow Crannell, a prominent anti from New York, suddenly dropped in on Spokane two days later. Elizabeth saw the editor of the *Chronicle* in the lobby of Hotel Spokane and explained with a smile that she had been so busy at home and with charities that she was arriving late to participate in the local discussion about giving women the right to vote.

The paper described this anti-suffragist as a large, well-built woman who was a bit past her prime. Never at a loss for words, she spoke easily and earnestly in conversation. And she put all of her verbal talents into identifying with women in Spokane who were opposed to the vote.

The anti-suffragist had not been at her own home very recently, however. Crannell had come to Washington from South Dakota, where thirty-eight cities had asked her to come speak. She had spoken all over the state but had put off many more invitations because she had told women in Washington—she did not specify which ones—that she would come to help their efforts to fight the amendment.

To Elizabeth's surprise, the train from South Dakota had stopped in Spokane on its way to Seattle. So, she had disembarked and was in the process of looking for fellow antis. She was here to help, she said, and she would not even ask for payment, except to cover her travel expenses. When the reporter pressed, Crannell said there were women in Spokane who had asked her to come, but she would not reveal their names. She planned to mail them her card and ask anyone interested to find her at the hotel.

The antis were afraid the amendment would pass in Washington, given that it had been written so that a simple majority of men voting for the amendment could make it become law. She explained that it would have been far less likely to pass if it had required a majority of all voters to pass it. Suffrage in Idaho and Colorado would never have been carried, she said, if those states had required a larger majority.

Almost a week after she arrived, Elizabeth happily told the *Chronicle* that she had found a large number of women opposed to suffrage in the city. And furthermore, they had been active, in a way she approved of. She claimed that the women had done such a good job that it would not be necessary for her to give a public speech there.

Crannell left Spokane soon afterward, refusing to give reporters the names of the local women who were opposed to voting. She insisted that she was willing to do so, but the ladies themselves were too private to have their names published. Before she left for Seattle, she told the reporter that she could receive telegrams at the Hotel Rainier Grand until the third of November.

In late October, Steeper happily announced that her partial canvass of the second ward had found four hundred women who wanted to vote and only fifteen who did not. She cautiously asserted that her poll was large enough to predict that the second ward would vote for the amendment.

During the final weeks before the election, Spokane was full of discussions about women voting. The local Protestant preachers met and voted 8–3 to support the amendment. On October 24, the *Chronicle* published several of their opinions on both sides of the subject.

The Reverend Jonathon Edwards, who would later publish an important history of early Spokane, told a reporter that he had carried a gun when he and his wife had gone to the polling stations to vote in 1884. He was happily surprised to see, however, that Spokane's male voters cleared a path for any woman who arrived at the polls, and even the saloonkeepers "realized that women were present and the election must be respectable."[16]

The next day, the priest presiding over Spokane's diocese reported that Catholic women were not interested in voting. He explained that his church had no doctrine to guide them as they decided how to vote on the subject. Then he stated that he did not favor suffrage because he had observed a jury with women and men on it, and he thought the women had taken far too much time to agree on a verdict.

During the last week before Washington's election, the *Chronicle* editor was still attempting to find out who the local anti-suffragists were. There were rumors from Seattle, where Elizabeth was still working, that they would soon organize into clubs. But even assurances that the paper would protect the identity of the antis did not bring any women out to identify themselves as anti-suffragists.

Only days before the election, a letter signed by Mrs. W.G. Piper, the wife of a prominent farmer in Idaho, appeared in the *Chronicle*. She said she feared that Crannell was working for the large liquor dealers in the region. Then she inquired, "What has become of her home while she is drifting so sadly away from it, way out west?"[17]

Despite insightful questions and "mean" tricks that demonstrated how intelligent Washington's suffragists were, most of the precincts in Spokane County voted against the measure. The small farming community of Rockford passed it, as did three other precincts. Forty-four others voted it down. Spokane was not as ready to allow women to vote.

18

MOVING ON

Lillie Steeper, the hardworking second ward suffragist who had found four hundred women who wanted to vote, was discouraged after the election. All of the precincts in that ward had voted against suffrage, demonstrating that just because many of the women who lived there supported the cause, it didn't mean their husbands, fathers and male friends were supportive.

However, Steeper and the local suffragists were glad that the *Chronicle* continued to publish news about the issue. One month after the election, the newspaper reported a suffrage "gain."[18] The paper claimed this even though the amendment had been defeated statewide by 10,326 votes. In Spokane County, the majority had been 1,501 against.

First, the reporter pointed out that the anti-suffragists, both local and statewide, had not organized. Second, the opposition to the amendment in 1898 was 40 percent less than it had been in 1889. The votes in favor had increased, while the votes against had decreased.

Spokane, however, had not been "gallant—not even a little bit."[19] Despite a gain in population of well over 15,000 since the previous vote, the city had fewer supporters of women voting in 1898 than it had nine years earlier. In 1889, county voters had cast 1,994 votes for the amendment. In 1898, voters cast only 1,743 votes for suffrage.

The *Chronicle* carried the subject of women voting into the new year. It published letters from Mrs. Homer Hill, the Seattle suffrage leader. And in late January 1899, she called a statewide meeting to be held in Seattle. The newspaper announced the event and invited local suffrage clubs to send delegates.

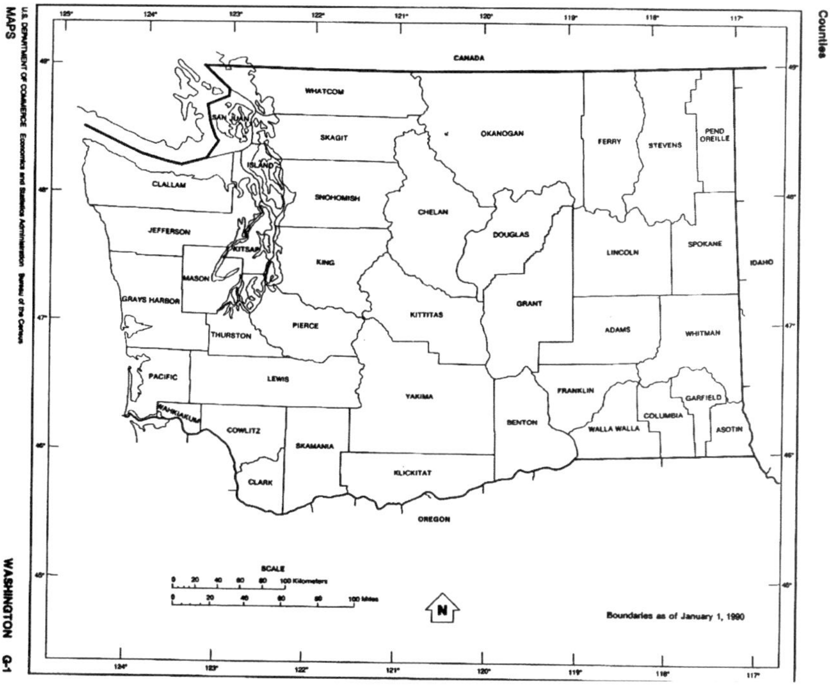

Washington bisected by the Cascade Mountains, divided east from west. *Courtesy of the Ned M. Barnes Room, Spokane Public Library.*

When no one from Spokane responded to the invitation, the *Chronicle* reported on the suffrage meeting and told where the delegates had come from. Walla Walla, in southeastern Washington, had sent representatives, as had Klickitat County in the central part of the state, but they were the sole participants from east of the Cascade Mountains.

In the early months of the year, a number of suffrage clubs throughout the state were regrouping and making plans to carry on an ongoing educational campaign to gain women's voting rights. The participating women wanted to constantly keep the subject in front of voters' minds. To do so, they needed to raise funds. The fact that suffrage campaigns were conducted in waves, as they had been so often, allowed voters to forget about the topic, making reorganizing for the next wave difficult.

In Spokane, women chose to focus on other issues. Reforming Spokane's saloon culture, cleaning the streets of drunkenness and prohibiting prostitution were a priority for some. Others continued to work toward establishing a police matron in local jails. It would take a strong and dedicated woman to bring suffrage back to the top of the local reform work.

19
TWENTIETH-CENTURY REFORM

In May 1901, Dr. P.S. Byrne was elected mayor on a promise to reform Spokane's politics. He sought to cut the city's expenditures by reducing the number of police and firemen employed and reducing payments made to city attorneys. Before he was sworn in, he also proposed adding a matron to the police department and asked the WCTU members to recommend a capable woman for the office. Most interested in cleaning up the saloon culture, he prohibited teens from frequenting the establishments and eventually oversaw a move to make selling alcohol to women illegal.

Most of the reforms that Mayor Byrne sought had been proposed by a group in Spokane that called themselves the Tax Reform League. The local Democratic caucus had incorporated the league's suggested reforms into their platform, and their choice for mayor, Byrne, had adopted them as his own.

The hiring of a police matron had not been proposed by the league, whose members were more concerned about women's behavior in the saloons than the living conditions in the jail. Byrne may well have adopted the idea from the WCTU, which he was in touch with that spring. He was the first Spokane politician to lend a respectful ear to requests for better treatment of women in jail.

The WCTU ladies recommended Elizabeth Tanner for the positon. She had long been active in church clubs and would later become the Salvation Army matron. Twenty women—who did not wish that their names be published in the paper—signed the petition for Tanner's appointment.

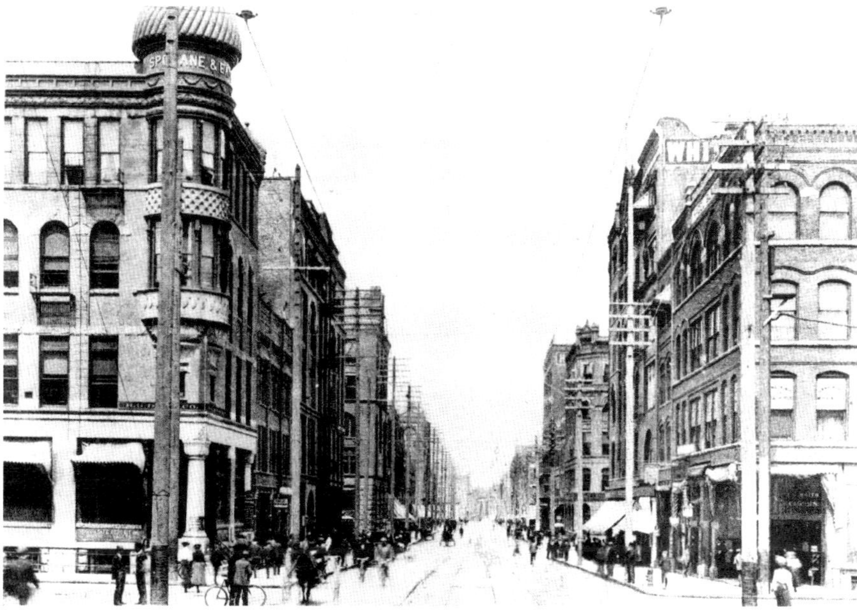

Howard Street was the heart of Spokane's business district at the turn of the twentieth century. *Courtesy of the Ned M. Barnes Northwest Room, Spokane Public Library.*

Their signatures complied with the 1893 law and made her a legal candidate for matron. Byrne miscalculated the support for a matron among the city council and found them not so enthusiastic as he had been. By October 1901, city council had defeated the ordinance for a police matron.

A year later, when a similar ordinance was more successful, Mayor Byrne announced that he would hire Salvation Army captain Vinnie Jost as a part-time police matron.[20] She had been helping women inmates at the local jail without remuneration for several months. When the city finally approved partial funding of a matron, Jost was the natural choice. She was well known in Spokane, and her name frequently appeared in the paper as an authority on women in jail. An on-call matron, she maintained her job with the Salvation Army and helped at the jail when requested.

For example, one day in the early 1890s, the police summoned Jost to come to the jail to assist a suicidal woman. The inmate, a mother of an unwed teen, had strangled her grandchild, fearing her family and friends would find out about her daughter's transgression. The grandmother confessed to the murder in court, telling the judge where the body of the baby could be found. After the trial, she was placed in prison. When she began banging her head on the wall of the cell, Jost went to the jail and spent part of a day and a night sitting with the despondent woman.

As the decade wore on, Captain Jost and a woman from the local Florence Crittenton Home—a mission that took in young women who were alone and often pregnant—became the spokespeople in Spokane for "fallen women." In 1904, the two called a meeting of club women at a local church.[21] They began speaking to a group of 150 women, trying to recruit new members for a reform league. By the time they were finished speaking, only 30 women were left—not enough to form a league.

By supporting a measure to prohibit the sale of alcohol to women, and by leaving before Jost's meeting was finished, the guests showed their disinterest in women whom they considered "fallen." They were very interested in helping poor mothers and babies or young single women who might fall into bad company. At the time, however, most of Spokane's club women were not interested in trying to reform the women who had already made bad choices and were spending time in saloons or had ended up in jail.

20

A SUFFRAGE LEADER IN THE MAKING

When twenty-three-year-old May Arkwright got off the train in North Idaho in 1883, she was on a quest to find her own life. A child born out of wedlock who claimed to be an orphan, she had grown up in the home of her blind grandfather in Youngstown, Ohio. She cooked for him at a young age, and when the two got the chance, they attended political meetings together. At one of these meetings, Arkwright had met a young attorney and the future president of the United States, William McKinley. The young woman was thrilled to make his acquaintance, and when he stayed overnight with her grandfather, she cooked a meal for the two men. Fascinated, she listened as McKinley and her grandfather discussed women's rights. The memory inspired her for the rest of her life.

As a young woman, she decided that the mining districts looked promising and got off the train when it stopped in North Idaho. She worked as a cook in a saloon until she had saved enough money to open her own boardinghouse. Arkwright soon made friends with the local miners and had the reputation of being the best cook in the area.

A young engineer who worked for the Northern Pacific Railroad, Levi W. Hutton, began stopping in at her kitchen for dinner as he made his way back and forth between the mines. The two shared the grief and loneliness of having grown up without parents and the adventure of being pioneers in North Idaho while still single. Their friendship grew, and they married in 1887.

They bought a small house in Wallace, Idaho, and soon after invested their savings in the Hercules Mine. A friend of theirs owned it, and he was determined to keep his claim out of the hands of large mine owners. The Huttons and their friends had little money, and they did most of the mining themselves, with picks and axes. For years, they went out to the claim to work in the evenings after they had finished their day jobs. They also spent weekends and holidays at the mine.

They struck a large vein of silver and lead in June 1901. Then they carried the ore out of the mine and down the mountainside in backpacks so that they could sell it and get enough money to buy mining machinery. The Huttons' original investment of little more than $5,000 netted them over $1 million.

The newly wealthy Huttons spent five more years in North Idaho. But Al (May's pet name for her husband) felt confined by the investment options and the political situation in North Idaho. May, always an independent thinker and her own person, did not get along well with the wealthy mine owners' wives in North Idaho.

In 1899, unrest among the miners had erupted, and a group of workers had hijacked Hutton's train at gunpoint, demanding that he take them to

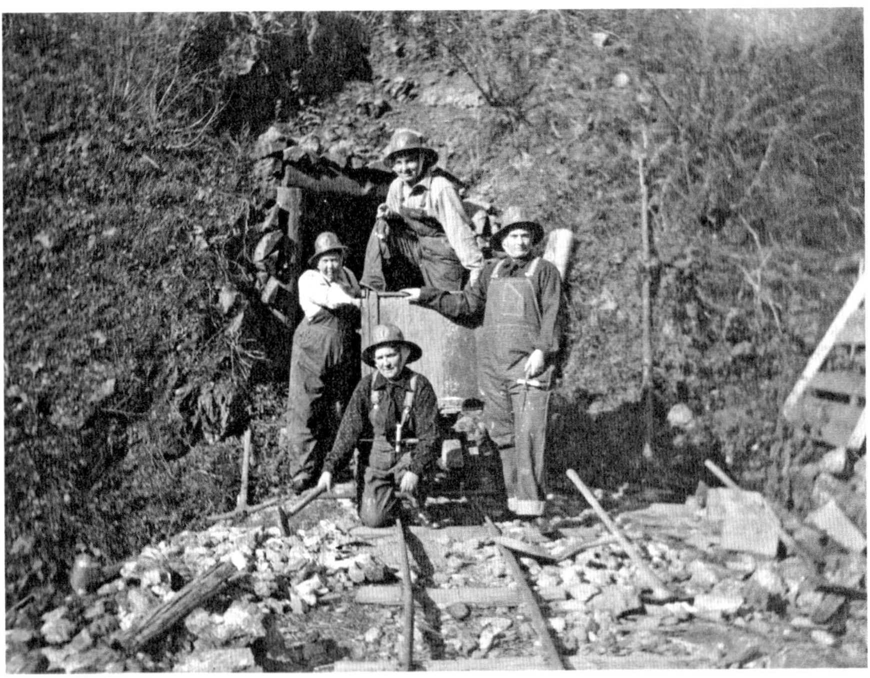

The Hercules miners pose in front of the mine. May Arkwright Hutton is on the back left. *Courtesy of the Eastern Washington State Historical Society: Museum of Arts and Culture.*

the Bunker Hill and Sullivan mines, where they set explosives. Authorities threw the whole batch of miners, along with Al Hutton, into the bullpen. May was incensed. She packed a lunch for Al and rushed down to the jail. Then she hounded the guards to let her in. She pestered the governor's representative so much that she eventually got Al released. She was still so angry, however, that she published a book—*The Coeur d'Alenes: Or, a Tale of the Modern Inquisition in North Idaho*—with the names of the characters only slightly changed, then called her book a novel. It was a lightly veiled attack on the mine owners.

Even after the Hercules made them rich, May, a new mine owner, did not find acceptance among the mine owners' wives. She was big and independent, and she enjoyed dressing in her own style, which could be boisterous and flamboyant. The refined women found her too rough for their own tastes. Even though May was now wealthy and thought she was their equal, the wives snubbed her.

However, being a mine owner gave May more options. She had always kept workers' interests and voting rights in her heart, and now she had money to help her favorite causes. Her new wealth gave her a broader stage on which to live and work.

While she claimed to her dying day to be proud of the book she had written, the reality was that the volume embarrassed the wealthy May. She bought as many of the remaining copies as she could find. This action effectively kept many from reading her indictment of the mine owners.

After some years, the couple decided to move to Spokane. Given the city's bigger population, Al would have more opportunities to make investments, and May could participate more fully in women's clubs. She had already occasionally traveled from North Idaho to Spokane to participate in suffrage meetings in the city.

In 1906, the Huttons purchased property on the corner of Washington Street and Sprague, where they built a four-story building. They transformed a large portion of the fourth floor of what became known as the Hutton Building into a roomy and comfortable apartment. They also bought a flashy red car—a favorite of May's.

The couple enjoyed living in Spokane. Al developed property, invested in the city and found many business opportunities. The Huttons' apartment, on Washington Street, was centrally located. May gave large dinner parties and befriended the children in the Home of the Friendless. She would drop by the home and take the children for a ride in her car, take them trinkets or provide parties for them. She joined the Woman's Hotel and made friends

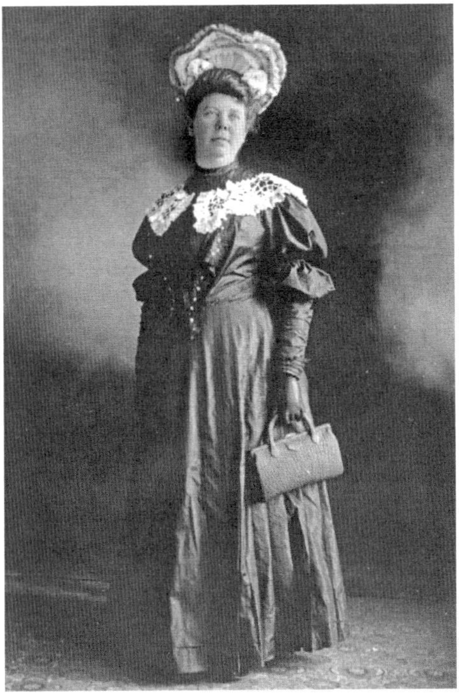

Right: May Arkwright Hutton enjoying one of her hats. *Courtesy of Washington State Archives.*

Below: Hutton joined the Woman's Hotel Club soon after she moved to Spokane. The friends pictured are probably Annie Durham (*left*) and La Reine Baker (*right*). *Courtesy of the Eastern Washington State Historical Society: Museum of Arts and Culture.*

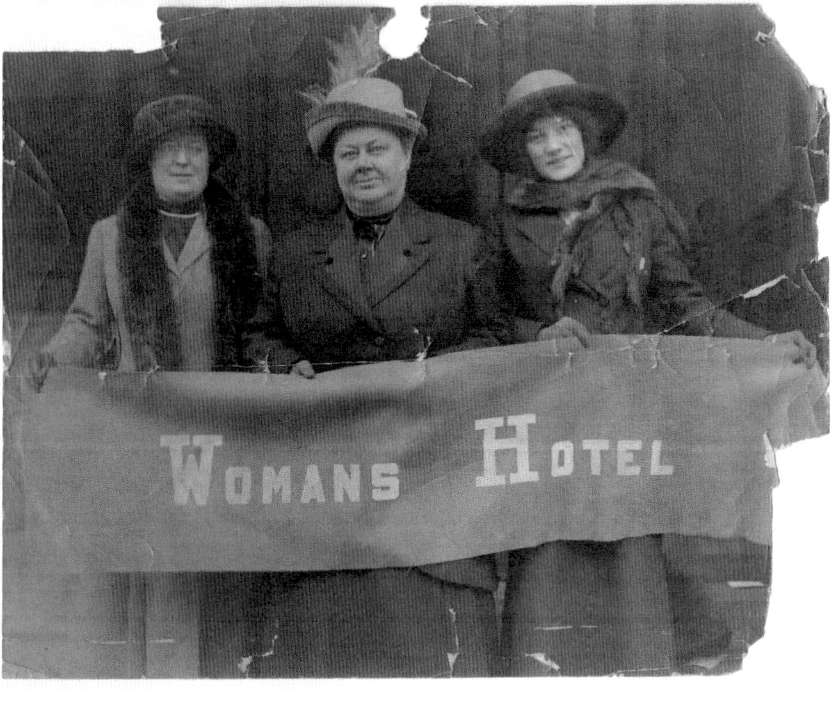

with Annie Durham, wife of the editor of the *Spokesman-Review*, and La Reine Helen Baker, a fellow mine owner who also advocated for suffrage. She adopted the Florence Crittenton Mission and spent time with the young ladies who lived there. She looked for men who would be willing to marry these young women. Then she bought the young ladies each a wedding dress and hosted their weddings in her apartment. And, perhaps best of all, living in Spokane gave her a place where she could play an important role in winning for Washington women the right to vote.

But part of May's heart stayed in Idaho. Many of the people who had mined with her and had eaten in her café still lived there. Because that state had enfranchised women in 1896, she had been voting there for ten years. In Washington, she felt discriminated against, and she felt as though her rights had been taken away from her. The thought made her feel insecure and despised.

Soon after she moved to Spokane, May found out she had another giant to face. She was diagnosed with Bright's disease, which would eventually take her life. All through the suffrage campaign she had to fight an ongoing bladder condition with sporadic bouts of nausea and fever.

Fortunately, when she was feeling well, she could usually shrug off feelings of insecurity. She could put on a fancy hat and head out to meet the world in her beloved car. Being out and talking to people lifted her spirits and inspired her best work. Spokane would soon have a bold-spirited and hardworking suffrage leader.

21

VOTES FOR WOMEN

By February 1908, the Huttons were completely settled in their fourth-floor apartment. May had joined several women's clubs, and Al was active in Spokane Chamber of Commerce, which kept rooms on a lower floor of the Hutton Building. One day, May was reading the *Chronicle* and found an article titled "Ask Voters to Give Women the Ballot."[22] She was looking for interesting newspaper clippings to keep in her scrapbooks and instantly knew she wanted that one to add to her collection.

The article announced that Emma Smith DeVoe had come to town to raise interest in a proposed amendment that would give women the right to vote in Washington. Hutton had long been active in suffrage organizations and had met the suffrage leader in Idaho more than ten years earlier while campaigning for women's voting rights in that state. She welcomed DeVoe's arrival and eagerly made plans with Al to attend the upcoming meeting on Saturday.

May was interested to note that DeVoe had organized several new suffrage clubs in western Washington beginning in September of the previous fall and that the statewide membership had more than tripled from 262 to 900. Confident that Spokane could add a significant number of members, she was eager to get involved and began making plans to attend the National American Woman's Suffrage Association's (NAWSA) annual meeting, in Seattle, in 1909.

That Saturday evening, Al and May hurried downstairs to the chamber of commerce rooms and participated in the meeting, which, having been

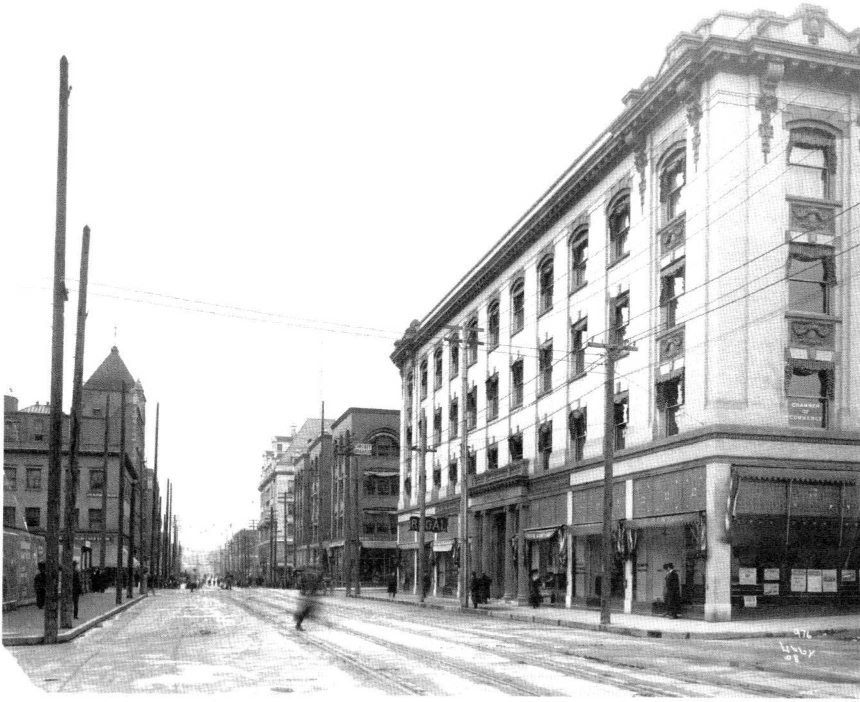

The Hutton Building, where the Huttons lived in the fourth-floor penthouse. *Courtesy of the Eastern Washington Historical Society: Museum of Arts and Culture.*

endorsed by the Woman's Club, was well attended. May was thrilled to learn how DeVoe had worked to create alliances for woman suffragists in Washington. The suffrage leader had been in touch with members of the state Grange organization, a politically activist group of farmers. The Grange, which had long given women leadership roles in its organization, was a natural for endorsing women's suffrage. Likewise, state labor organizations supported the cause. Moreover, Emma told her listeners that the amendment would get support from the state's sizable population of Scandinavian immigrants. Since Norway, Finland and Denmark had already given women voting rights, she argued, people who came from these countries—who made up more than one-quarter of the state's population—would support the cause.

During the meeting, suffragists organized a Spokane branch of the Washington State Equal Suffrage Association. They elected May president, and forty people joined the group. May and Emma told reporters after the meeting that they hoped to have one local hundred members within a few days. Then they issued a general invitation to all who were interested, both women and men, to come to a reception for DeVoe on the following Monday evening.

At the reception, DeVoe appointed Hutton to present the Washington State suffragists' viewpoint to Congress on March 3, 1908. The *Chronicle* announced that Hutton would be going to the nation's capital and told its readers that she had made a thorough study of the issue. It added that Washington was to be congratulated in having Hutton as a representative.[23]

By Monday night, Spokane's suffrage group had doubled to eighty members. The growing numbers of suffragists energized May. She loved making friends and was happy to see their numbers increasing. The busier she got, the better she felt about living in Spokane.

Hutton was initially glad to know that DeVoe chaired the statewide organization, but the two women had their differences. Emma prized ladylike behavior and taught that the best way for women to win the right to vote was for them to be quietly friendly with everyone and to shrink away from any behavior that might be confrontational or might irritate voters or lawmakers. For example, she argued that voting would help women guard their homes. It would not take them out of their homes—their most important place of influence—as many anti-suffragists argued. Rather, being able to vote would help them be better mothers. She described the way she went about gaining the right to vote as a "still hunt."

Hutton agreed that women suffragists should wage a "still hunt." But May could never be as ladylike as Emma was every day. She was as comfortable in a pair of overalls, working with a pick in the Hercules mine, as she was wearing more feminine clothing. Wearing a dress and hat were fun, and May liked to be loud with friends.

Hutton's "still hunt" was less about behaving properly and more about having one-on-one conversations with voters regarding women's right to vote. She believed that developing relationships in a parlor would be more effective than speaking to a large gathering. Once a friend looked at you and told you he would vote for suffrage, she said, you could count on him to follow through. On the other hand, fifty people might listen to you make a speech but never get around to voting for suffrage.

Both women put their hearts and long hours into the cause. Both wanted the same ends. However, their devotion to their shared goal outlasted their friendship.

22
SPOKANE'S "STILL HUNT"

After DeVoe left in late February 1908, May continued working to get the vote. But few traces of her work could be found in local newspapers. Occasional announcements of meetings appeared, but otherwise, the effort to gain signatures for petitions and increase the numbers of suffragists in Spokane was waged away from the public eye.

May enjoyed hosting parties in her spacious apartment, during which she would serve her guests home-cooked specialties and take the time to get acquainted with them. She would introduce her work as the president of Spokane's chapter of the Washington Equal Suffrage League and encourage her guests to sign a petition.

She sometimes pulled speech material from others' speeches, putting her own spin on well-worn suffrage arguments. One of the points she liked to make was that legally preventing women from voting pushed them into a class with "idiots and criminals." She then would state, "Women are your intellectual, moral and social equals and should be your political equals as well."[24]

Another favorite theme she emphasized was that "taxation without representation exists in Washington." She argued that there was little ideological difference between what was happening in 1908 and the events that surrounded the Boston Tea Party in colonial America.

May would make her listeners laugh when she refuted the argument that giving women the right to vote would also require them to sit on juries. She would explain, "I think women who stand behind counters or in factories, at a cook stove, wash tub, ironing table, dish sink and baby crib, would be glad to sit on almost anything for a rest."[25]

But giving public speeches was not her first choice for promoting suffrage. If there was someone else in town who would give the speeches for her, she would happily let them. Sometimes, these were women from Spokane, and sometimes they were suffragists from Seattle. In November 1908, DeVoe came back to Spokane, and Hutton made appointments for her to speak as many as three times a day. May happily reported to Emma that Spokane was piling up the signatures by the hundreds and predicted she would have a very nice showing when she got to Olympia in mid-January 1909.

Even though she happily scheduled speaking appointments for Emma, May was following her own ideas for promoting suffrage. Writing to a friend in Seattle, she bragged a little. The Seattle suffragist had complained that she was bone-tired from posting "Votes for Women" signs all over the city. Hutton responded, "I have less than a ton [of suffrage signs] in cold storage, and will use them when we are ready for the men to vote on the question. In my opinion, these posters in the face of the people at this time only arouses antagonism."[26]

May and Emma clashed on many different ideas. May was especially irritated by frequent requests for money from suffragists working from the west side of the state. By late 1908, several women were expecting that May and her wealthy friend La Reine Baker would be the primary funding sources for their suffrage campaigns. May was willing to give some money, and had done so over the summer, but by November, she was drawing the line on new requests.

On the other hand, the Seattle suffragists had struggled since the 1880s to raise enough money to fund their campaigns. In 1908, when they heard that a handful of wealthy woman suffragists were active on the east side of the mountains, it was very tempting for them to flood Hutton and Baker with requests for donations. May responded that Spokane's entire suffrage campaign was dependent on her own and Baker's resources and that the two women were not willing to be the sole financial sources for the Seattle campaigns as well.

By the time she got extra petitions in the mail from Seattle, she had already made up her own. So she decided the best thing to do with the extras was to take them to the heads of the labor organizations based in Spokane. This laid the groundwork for closer cooperation between the suffragists and the labor organizations in the future.

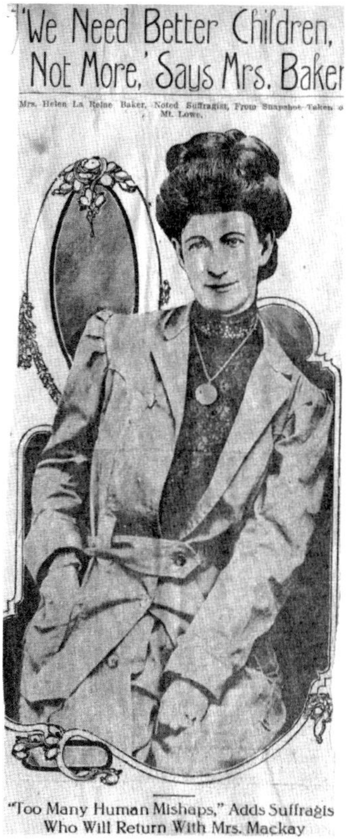

'We Need Better Children, Not More,' Says Mrs. Baker

Mrs. Helen La Reine Baker, Noted Suffragist, From Snapshot Taken o Mt. Lowe.

"Too Many Human Mishaps," Adds Suffragis Who Will Return With Mrs. Mackay

La Reine Helen Baker. *Courtesy of the Eastern Washington State Regional Archives: Museum of Arts and Culture.*

The Spokane Woman's Club invited Hutton to speak to them on November 16, 1908. Hutton enjoyed working with the Woman's Club. The suffrage campaign was winning her new respect. Many of Spokane's club women admired her for what she was accomplishing.

At the same time, La Reine Baker was creating her own speaking appointments. For example, she bought two hundred pairs of mittens for orphans in Spokane and then invited some of her neighbors to come help crochet fancy borders on the mittens. While they were there, the ladies asked Baker to speak to them about suffrage. She succeeded so well that ten of the ladies who had helped her marched "down and registered to vote in the school elections."[27]

Baker was helping to get the written word out about suffrage. She and Hutton had decided that one of the best ways to do so was to publish articles in local papers. La Reine began writing weekly columns and sending them to Sunday papers throughout the region. May told Emma that the articles were appearing in twenty-five papers and that the articles had made more converts to the cause than anything she had done.

In December 1908, Billy Sunday, the popular Christian evangelist, arrived in Spokane and began a crusade. News of ten thousand people attending his meetings reached Seattle. And soon Hutton heard rumors from Seattle suggesting that the large numbers of suffrage petitioners coming from Spokane were not reflective of their interest in women getting the vote—they were there due to the religious frenzy stirred up by Sunday.

Hutton was infuriated at the slight. She sent to Seattle a copy of an editorial published in Spokane before Sunday arrived, showing the large response that she had found while encouraging women to sign up to vote in the upcoming school elections. Miffed, May sent a warning to Seattle: "Tell them not to make the fatal political mistake of trifling with the present wishes of the people, for if they do they will be left so far in the rear they won't get the smoke and cinders dug out of their eyes for years to come."

Despite her growing frustration with DeVoe's leadership, Hutton kept working with the Seattle suffragists. Emma came back to Spokane in mid-December to hold three more days of meetings. While she was in town, she spoke at the chamber of commerce, Cliff Park Social Club, Spokane College and the Swedish Tabernacle. Between meetings, La Reine Baker entertained DeVoe, Hutton and other suffragists.

In January, Baker and Hutton attended state equal suffrage meetings in Olympia, scheduled to coincide with the legislative session. The group met in the state's capitol, planning to encourage the legislators to support their goal of getting the proposed amendment on the 1910 ballot. After Hutton got home, she wrote to a friend, saying that the weeks she had spent in Olympia were the most strenuous of her life. It proved a changing point for Hutton as well.

23

THE OLYMPIA CAMPAIGN

On January 15, the Huttons and the Bakers took the train to Olympia, Washington's capital, for the statewide suffrage meeting. They stopped in Seattle for a day before traveling to Olympia, where the rest of the state's suffrage representatives were gathering. May and La Reine, along with their husbands for part of the time, took up residence in the Hotel Mitchell near the capitol building. The rest of the suffragists stayed in a house that the Washington Equal Rights Association (WERA) had rented.

May shipped her red car to Olympia—the trans-Washington roads were not developed enough at the time to allow a person to easily drive across the state—and paid her trusted driver to come with her on the trip. She explained to the *Chronicle* that it was a winning car; she had brought it along for good luck. This decision to take her car felt right to May but did not go over so well with the Seattle suffragists, who thought she should have left her car at home and put the extra money into their side of the campaign.

DeVoe put Hutton in charge of delivering signed petitions to specific members of the legislature. The Spokane suffrage leader had excelled at gathering signatures, and it was a natural choice to let her make sure the petitions were properly delivered. It also preserved the task of lobbying for Emma and her handpicked assistants, women and men, who kept up a friendly but constant effort reminding legislators that they wanted them to support the proposed amendment on voting rights.

To complement this measure, DeVoe hired publicity agents to write daily news releases, which they sent to newspapers all over the state. On January

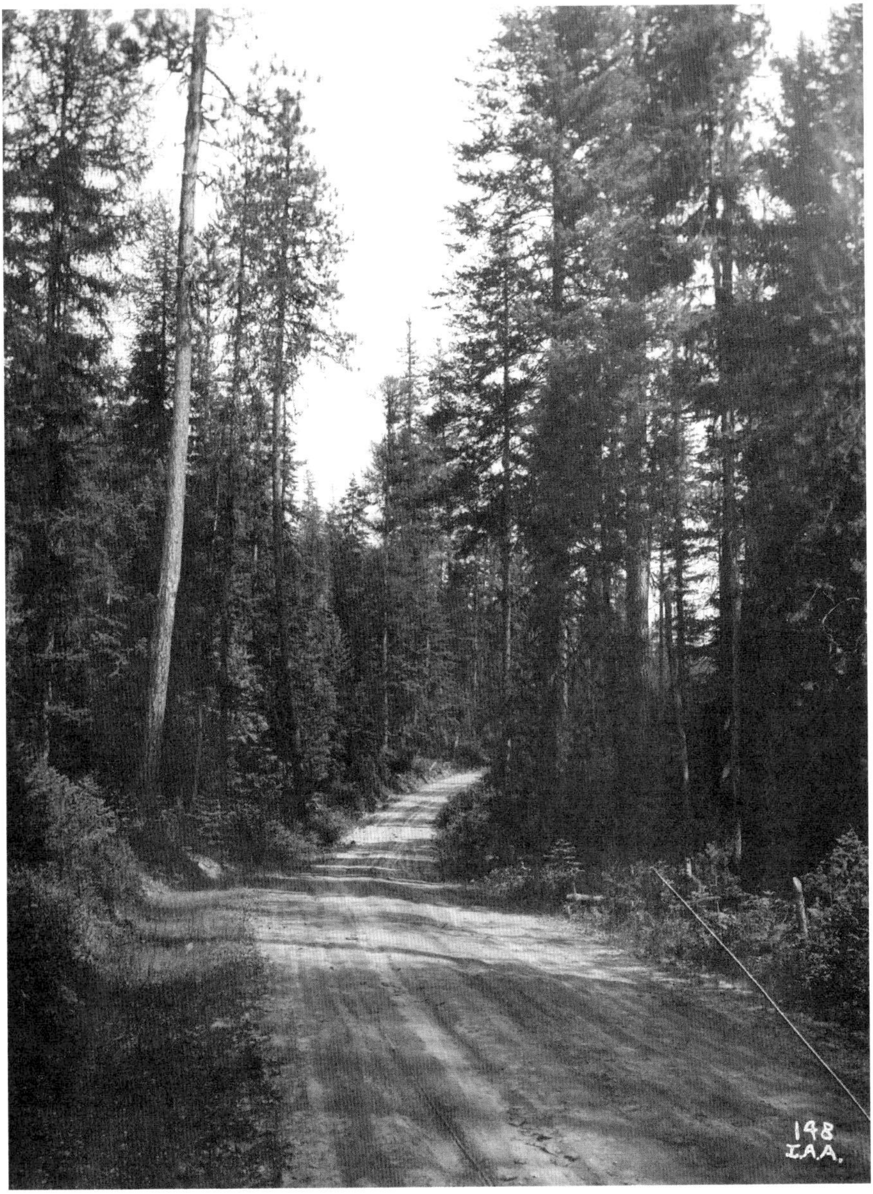

Roads were often unmarked and only passable in good weather. *Courtesy of the Ned M. Barnes Northwest Room, Spokane Public Library.*

16, the *Chronicle* predicted that Spokane women might be voting in the primaries in the upcoming spring elections. The paper explained that the suffragists were hoping to add a constitutional amendment to the ballot. If they could not gain enough support for that, they had two other options, one of which was to seek women's right to vote in primaries.

Another thing going for the suffragists was that a local option tax on alcohol was being voted on. The *Chronicle* put it succinctly when it speculated that the suffragists' most powerful opponents—the alcohol lobby—would not have time to oppose both the tax and women's suffrage. Emma and her allies had done such a good job of separating their cause from temperance that liquor interests did not try to delete the measure.

Hutton and DeVoe rejoiced when the constitutional amendment on voter qualifications was introduced on January 20. After the amendment had been allowed a brief time on the floor, supporters reassigned it to a more favorable subcommittee. Nine days later, the House of Representatives approved the amendment.

The suffragists had done their work well. The *Chronicle* reported that seventy had voted yes, eighteen had voted no and seven had not voted. It was a slim margin, only three votes more than the required two-thirds vote. But it was all the bill needed to move on to the Senate. A feather specifically for Hutton's cap was the fact that every member of the Spokane delegation had voted for the measure.

The path through the Senate was harder. As soon as the bill was proposed, a Seattle senator voted to postpone it. But a supporter reassigned it once again, this time into a committee with more sympathetic members. The setback disappointed suffragists, especially Hutton, who had her heart set on going home with the news that the amendment would be on the ballot. Instead, the legislative session was due to close soon, with the bill stuck in a committee.

May wanted to push the bill all the way through and was not afraid to say so. She cornered a senator who was a suffragist and demanded that he submit the bill immediately. Emma and her allies were horrified and began preparing to blame Hutton for killing the amendment before it reached the Senate. One Seattle suffragist later claimed May had used inappropriate language in front of the legislators and had offered to buy a senator's vote.[28]

DeVoe insisted that it was best to continue gently lobbying the senators who would be voting on the amendment. They would do so until they had a two-thirds majority to support the bill in the Senate. Emma's allies from Seattle planned to pull another petition together and present it to a Seattle senator who publicly opposed the measure.

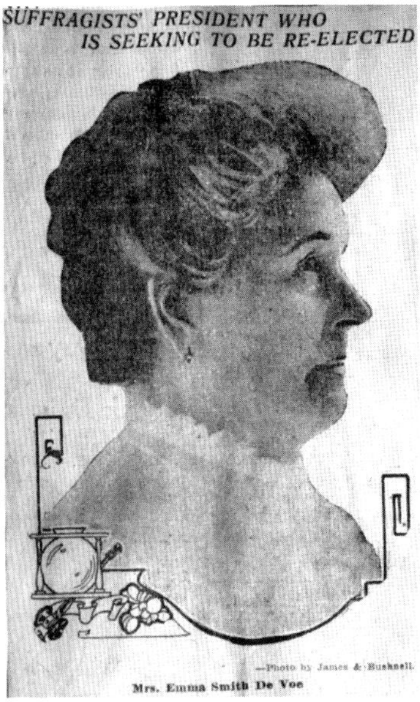

Emma Smith DeVoe was an important suffrage leader in Washington. *Courtesy of the Eastern Washington State Regional Archives: Museum of Arts and Culture.*

Despite their differences with DeVoe, Hutton and Baker stayed in Olympia until late February. May wrote to a friend the day after she returned home, saying that she expected the amendment to pass the Senate shortly after 2:00 p.m. that day. And she proudly added that there had been a lot of bright women lobbying for it. A *Chronicle* headline that evening ran, "Women May Soon Vote."

The next day, a happy and smiling group of suffragists sat in the Senate gallery and watched House bill no. 59 pass without any additional amendments. When the amendment passed, the ladies politely waved their handkerchiefs. Then DeVoe and friends picked up the bill and walked it to the governor's office for his signature.

That night, the *Chronicle* published kudos to May Arkwright Hutton, who "directed the work of the female lobby until the victory was assured."[29] If not exactly correct describing what she had done, it was a warm welcome home for the exhausted Hutton. She would need the encouragement for the weeks to come.

But she could not rest on her laurels. When she got home, the real work was waiting. She now had to persuade Spokane's male voters that women deserved the right to vote.

24

BUSIEST JAY IN SPOKANE

In early March 1909, Hutton was being congratulated on every side. Spokane's residents credited her with pushing the amendment through Olympia. They hardly cared what DeVoe and her supporters had done.

But May was not one to sit back and take it easy. She had to get busy. There was an election to win. And since La Reine Baker, her right-hand helper, had left from Olympia on a trip that eventually took her to the Fourth Conference of the International Woman Suffrage Alliance in London, May had to do double duty.

She began putting her best efforts into recruiting members for the Spokane branch of WERA. She scheduled activities to be held around town, including at two colleges, Blair Business and Gonzaga, and at the North Side High School. She began a contest, complete with monetary prizes, for the best essay responding to the prompt "Why women should be given the ballot." She also set out to write articles to replace the ones Baker had been sending to twenty papers throughout eastern Washington.

In addition, she held a parlor suffrage meeting every day, campaigned for a friend who was running for mayor and ordered a gavel made of wood harvested from the four states that had granted women the vote. When she found out that she had been eliminated from the roster of speakers for the upcoming suffrage convention, she wrote to Mrs. Homer Hill, a Seattle suffrage friend, and offered to let her use the gavel.

By early April, May was stretched too thin. So she decided to recuperate at a nearby hot springs. She wrote to La Reine that she would be going away to relax for ten days but said she had invited two of her Seattle suffrage friends to join her. They would spend their time at the springs laying plans for a ten-day campaign that May said would "make this old town to sit up and take notice."[30]

While Spokane was humming with suffrage activity, Hutton's relationship with DeVoe and her allies was deteriorating. Hutton got a letter in early May threatening to "eliminate her entirely from the suffrage work" in Washington if she did not comply with Emma's wishes.[31] Friends informed her that the Seattle suffrage leader was scheming to destroy everything Hutton had done. The threats bothered May briefly—they simply encouraged her to work harder to promote women's voting rights in her own way.

By late May, Hutton's suffrage club had five hundred members. A friend and longtime political activist, David C. Coates—who had known May when they both lived in Wallace—insisted that the group needed one thousand members by the end of June. That way they could be properly represented when they attended the National American Woman's Suffrage Convention scheduled for Seattle in early July. In other words, May would need a large retinue so that it would be difficult for DeVoe to prevent them from participating.

In efforts to reach her lofty membership goals, Hutton even sent a few letters granting honorary memberships. One of these was to the wife of the mayor in Tekoa, Washington. Three others were to a family who now lived in Seattle, whom Hutton wished to make delegates to the upcoming suffrage convention.

While branching out, Hutton and her allies began organizing different clubs, including a college suffrage club and a stenographers' club. The women also held parlor meetings, both in Spokane and in nearby towns and cities. In one afternoon, Sarah Commerford, president of the College Equal Suffrage Club, organized North Kenwood and Opportunity, Washington.

The delegates for the NAWSA convention in Seattle planned to travel from New York to Seattle on a "Suffrage Special train." The chartered train would make campaign-like stops across the United States, during which suffragists would make speeches about women voting, from a platform at the back of the train. Hutton knew that the train would go right through Spokane, so she began making plans to entertain the national delegates.[32]

May and Al Hutton asked the chamber of commerce for a $300 grant to entertain the national officers while they were in Spokane. They would honor them, along with La Reine Baker, at a banquet, and would present to Anna Howard Shaw a gavel made of wood cut in the four suffrage states.

Mayor Nelson Pratt, whom Hutton had supported in the general election, would also give a speech. May even wrote a letter to the Northern Pacific Railway to find out how much time the national delegates would have in Spokane. When she found out that they would be in the city for several hours on June 28, she happily wrote to Baker saying she was sure she could show the national officers that she was still part of the Washington suffrage scene.

On June 10, two days before the membership lists were due, May's group included five hundred legitimate members and represented five clubs. She wrote to Seattle suffragists and enclosed a check for $100.00 in dues for four hundred members of her own club. In addition, she sent $3.50 from the College Equal Suffrage Club, $7.00 from the Kenwood Club, $4.50 from the Opportunity Club and $3.50 from the Stenographers' Club, for an additional total of $18.50.

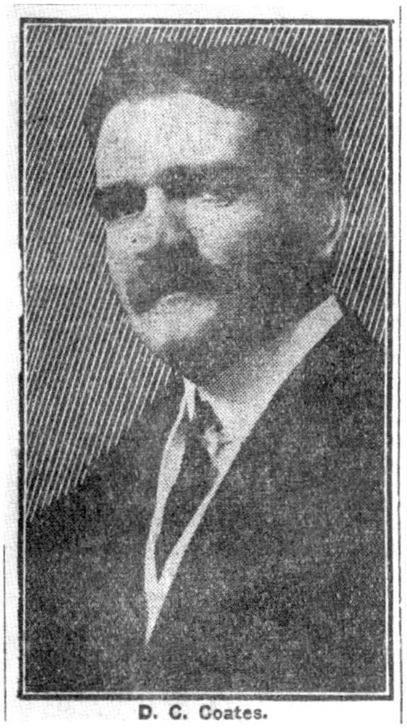

David C. Coates was a socialist, activist and friend of Hutton's. *Courtesy of the Washington State Eastern Regional Branch.*

Hutton eagerly planned entertainment for the national officers. It would include good food, a tour of the city, swimming and suffrage speeches. May wrote to the national officers, "The special is to arrive in Spokane at 8 a.m. June 28th, and leave at 2:30 a.m. on the 29th. This will give us time to carry out our program."

She acknowledged that she had planned "a pretty full day," but added, "I think we are equal to it. The Chamber of Commerce is assisting the local club, which now numbers 500 members, in entertaining these guests. Please send me names of all prominent people who are coming so that we may use them in the newspapers and attract attention and get out a big crowd. Also, please wire me when your train leaves Livingston, Montana, so that I may have time to prepare breakfast."

June 28 dawned bright and clear. Eighty-five women from all over the United States and Canada arrived early. The national officers enjoyed one of Hutton's famed breakfasts in her apartment. Then the visitors enjoyed chauffeured car tours of the city and a refreshing dip in a pool. The highlight of the day was a banquet at the Davenport Hotel, where Hutton presented the gavel to the national president and Emma Smith DeVoe toasted the visiting officers. Mayor Pratt welcomed them to the city and then declared himself a suffragist, to the ladies' delight. The evening hours left time for an open suffrage meeting from the back of the train.

The day was a resounding success for Hutton and for the city. When the suffrage train rolled on, the delegates carried with them a grand impression of Spokane and its hospitality. It was a fabulous experience that would linger in their minds for years to come—and impressed Spokane voters as well.

25
SMOKE, CINDERS AND SUFFRAGE

The calm between Hutton and DeVoe that allowed Spokane's entertainment to be such a success fell apart shortly after the suffragists arrived in Seattle. When the Spokane delegation attempted to register for the Washington State convention—which preceded the national convention—the chair of the credentials committee, Cora Smith Eaton, refused them. She charged that Hutton had paid for some of the delegates to come to the convention in Seattle and argued this would disqualify her team.

Hutton had come to the convention with a clear conscience, and she did not believe she had done anything wrong. She had invited her friends to join the Spokane delegation, even paid for a few. She also had offered trips to the Seattle convention as prizes for selected students who lived in Spokane. In the weeks before she went to Seattle, May had taken special pains to make sure that all the constituents of her suffrage league and the delegates from Spokane were legitimate members. She had been so sure that they were all in good standing that she had written to Baker just before she sent the memberships in to the Washington Equal Suffrage Association and explained with relief that she thought no one could question her delegates. But the way she had done so left the door open for these accusations.

Eaton was at least technically correct in her suspicion. However, she was also angry about Hutton's earlier refusals to fund more expenses of the west side suffragists. She had also accused Hutton of using bad language in the capitol in 1908. But she was intensely loyal to DeVoe, and the real reason she did not want to seat the Spokane delegation was that she disliked and distrusted Hutton. She accused May of habitually using profane and obscene language and claimed that she had evidence that Hutton's activities in Idaho had been inappropriate, even implying that she had fostered prostitution.

Hutton had come from a very different background. She talked more boisterously than DeVoe and Eaton did. Furthermore, her activities in Idaho had included publishing an inflammatory book against the mine owners, which Hutton had tried to suppress after she made her fortune.

Eaton claimed magnanimously that she would not pass along the information she had about Hutton, if Hutton would not push to have her delegates seated. Apparently, blackmail was more acceptable to Eaton than allowing suspect delegates to vote.

If the Spokane delegates had been the only ones denied seating, Eaton's accusations might appear credible. She had refused, however, to seat twenty-two other clubs as well. Clearly, she and DeVoe were protecting their territory and ridding it of people they did not wish to keep in their group.

The forty-nine delegates from Spokane, including Baker and Hutton—who were members of the executive committee and would have been allowed to go in without their voting privileges—were herded into a small side room in Plymouth Congregational Church. The crowded group was asked to stay there until the officers of the Washington State Equality Club had been elected.

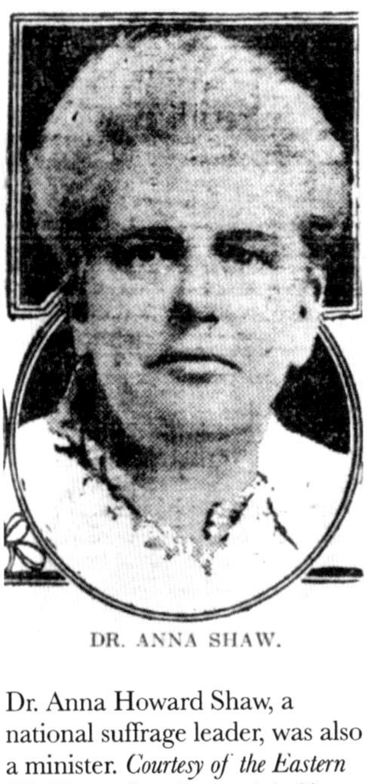

DR. ANNA SHAW.

Dr. Anna Howard Shaw, a national suffrage leader, was also a minister. *Courtesy of the Eastern Washington State Regional Archives: Museum of Arts and Culture.*

The ousted delegates did not stay in one place long. DeVoe allies herded them, like cattle, from room to room. At one point, they were crowded into a small room with no water. Finally, the members of Hutton's delegation, who had hung on to a sense of humor, took matters into their own hands. With the help of Coates, Hutton and Baker investigated a window in the back of the room. They found it was unlocked and on the ground floor. Then Coates helped the delegation escape through the window.[33]

Anna Howard Shaw, the national president, was irritated by the squabble and refused to seat DeVoe at the national convention. She also told the Seattle leader that if she wanted to keep her position as a paid organizer for

NAWSA, she would have to reconcile with Hutton. DeVoe refused to do so and never again worked for Shaw or cooperated with Hutton.[34]

A subdued Hutton arrived back in Spokane with Baker on July 10. She talked to a *Chronicle* reporter only after her friend, Baker, stopped to talk. But when she did, her courage returned, and she declared, "My name hasn't spelled defeat yet and I propose to have it spell success in the future."[35]

Hutton noted that DeVoe had created her own problems. She then proposed that suffragists of Washington establish a new organization that would meet in Spokane in October. But Hutton declared that she would not seek the presidency of the new group; if the members decided they did not want her to be president, she would be happy to take her car out and organize the common people throughout the state.

Baker followed up by saying that they planned to invite every man and woman in the state over the age of fifteen to an event in Spokane, to be held October 10–17. This proposed group would already be a member of the national suffrage association because she and Hutton had had it approved by the national officers while they were still in Seattle.

The smoke and cinders in Seattle damaged the state's suffrage movement only momentarily. The division created more suffrage institutions both in Seattle and in Spokane. The campaign to make Washington a free state would move on toward Election Day.

26
CAMPAIGN EXPERIMENTS

Hutton regrouped quickly after returning from Seattle. Several men had become interested in organizing for suffrage after seeing the suffrage train come through Spokane. In addition, May's friend and co-worker La Reine Baker wanted to try out some of the strategies that she had learned during her visit to the World Suffrage Conference in London.

The two friends decided to combine La Reine's idea of an open-air meeting with a Spokane summertime theme. So, they established Camp Equality with four tents on the tree-lined shores of Liberty Lake, just sixteen miles east of Spokane. On July 13, the ladies loaded a car with clothes, pens, paper and suffrage materials, along with a maid, a cook and a boat driver, and headed for camp. They announced that there would be a mass meeting of suffragists from eastern Washington on the following Sunday. Everyone interested in women voting was invited to bring a basket lunch and play in the morning. In the afternoon, they would hold a mass suffrage meeting.

The following Sunday, Hutton and her team met at Camp Equality. After they had all played around on the water and enjoyed picnic lunches, May called the meeting. David Coates and La Reine helped. May told the story of the Seattle convention and explained why their delegation had been treated as insurgents. She also revealed why she and her fellow leaders had decided to break with DeVoe's group and establish their own organization. The rest of the meeting was occupied with plans for a convention in Spokane in October. In the intervening months, the allies planned to send out representatives to every county in Washington to invite them to the meeting.

On July 24, the *Chronicle* announced the Spokane suffragist camp. It went on to say the women had official permission to hold open-air suffrage meetings in Spokane on Monday nights for a month. May and her associates publicized the camp far and wide. Two days later, the *Ottawa Citizen*, based east of the Great Lakes in Canada, announced that a suffragists' camp was in session at picturesque Liberty Lake.[36]

The camp did not last too long after the big meeting. By that time, Hutton's forces had shifted tactics. They were going to try holding open-air park meetings. La Reine, who was the main instigator of the meetings, told May that they were fortunate to have permission to hold these meetings. May was less enthusiastic, but she lent her name to the cause at first.

The suffragists held their first meeting in Manito Park on Spokane's South Hill. David Coates officiated. Baker and a friend from the College Equal Suffrage Club, Mrs. Z.W. Commerford, were the speakers. May went but was offended when one of the speakers reacted harshly to a group of noisy children nearby. She worried that the parents of the children had been turned off and wondered how much good the meeting was doing.

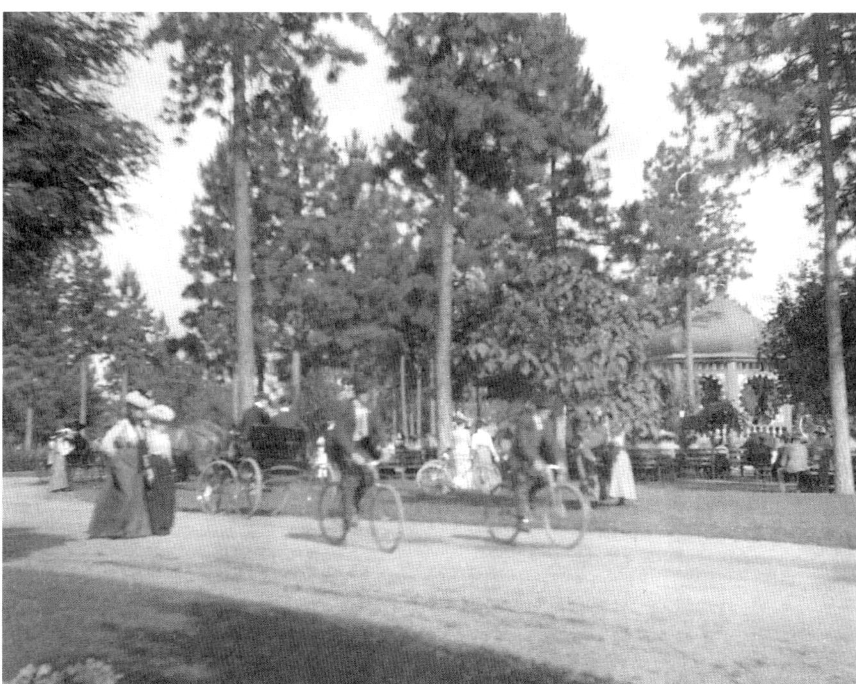

Spokane residents enjoying a stroll in Coeur d'Alene Park. *Courtesy of the Ned M. Barnes Northwest Room, Spokane Public Library.*

La Reine was excited about the park meetings. She continued to work with Commerford and with a Seattle suffragist. They were holding meetings several nights a week in different parks around the city. La Reine even got permission to speak during the intermissions of band concerts.

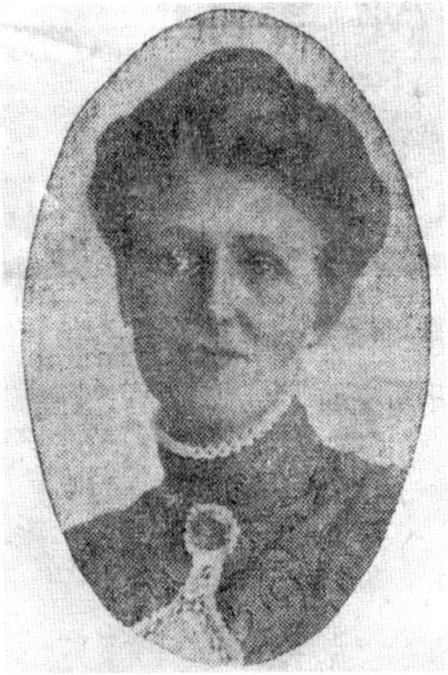

Sarah Commerford was president of the College Equal Suffrage Club. *Courtesy of the Eastern Washington State Historical Society: Museum of Arts and Culture.*

The *Spokesman-Review*, often critical of the campaign for women to vote, reported on Saturday, July 30, that the park meetings were popular.[37] Large crowds had attended nightly. The third event they had put on had been the most effective to date, with four hundred people attending.

May was not impressed. The second meeting that she attended was one that she had arranged for the speaker, Governor Varsey of South Dakota, whose own state had a suffrage amendment pending voter approval. He was in town attending an irrigation congress. May contacted him and invited him to speak. He agreed and spoke for thirty minutes to an audience of approximately two thousand people. His remarks were well received. But still Hutton wondered how effective the meetings were.[38]

Despite May's growing consternation, La Reine continued to hold open-air meetings. On August 17, she spoke to a crowd of 1,500 people at Liberty Park. She spoke again the following night, at Corbin Park. The meetings continued, frequently pulling in large numbers.

By September 23, May had made up her mind. She wrote to a friend in Seattle, "I have succeeded in putting the kibosh on any more park or street meetings in Spokane."[39] She explained that she thought the methods they were using were militant. Comparing the Spokane meetings to what suffragists were doing in England, she concluded, "It is my opinion that it is an insult to American Manhood."

She further explained her misgivings about the open-air meetings in a letter she wrote to Abigail Scott Duniway, stating, "You know, just as soon as we begin an openly aggressive campaign, the elements that organized against you in Oregon will organize against us."[40]

May's decision to ask the city to revoke their approval of the open-air meetings led to further fracturing of the suffragists' cohesion. A few days after they had to stop holding the meetings, Baker and Commerford pulled out of May's new Suffrage League. The younger women decided Hutton's group was too conservative for them. Thus Baker, although she had been elected a delegate to Hutton's meeting, said that she would have too much to do to attend the October convention.

27

SEATTLE IS HERE WITH NO BILLS

The audience laughed heartily when Leonia Brown, a Seattle delegate and president of a suffrage club there, announced that "Seattle is here with no bills!" It was a humorous reference to the difficulties that May had experienced leading up to the Seattle convention. Leonia had served since July as the temporary secretary of the "insurgent" suffrage organization that had grown out of the Seattle convention.

Leonia brought with her a draft of a constitution to use as they established the new group, thereby providing a key document for the day. Before the day was over, she would be voted first vice president of the executive committee in charge of the west-side group.

The meeting had just begun in Spokane's Masonic Temple, downtown on Riverside Street. The women and men there were establishing May's new suffrage organization independently of any other similar leagues. Approximately fifty people were there for the event, despite the last-minute departures of Baker and her College Club friends.

May was sticking to the promise she had made on July 10 when she told a reporter that she was willing to let someone else lead. If the suffragists thought they needed a different leader, she said, she was willing to step back from leadership and take her car out recruiting. Thus, Brown and Carrie Hill had been selected as the temporary leaders of the new group; they would also moderate the voting that day.

Earlier in the week, May and her fellow organizers had decided that they could finish the tasks at hand in one day. Thus, on Friday, October 8, they

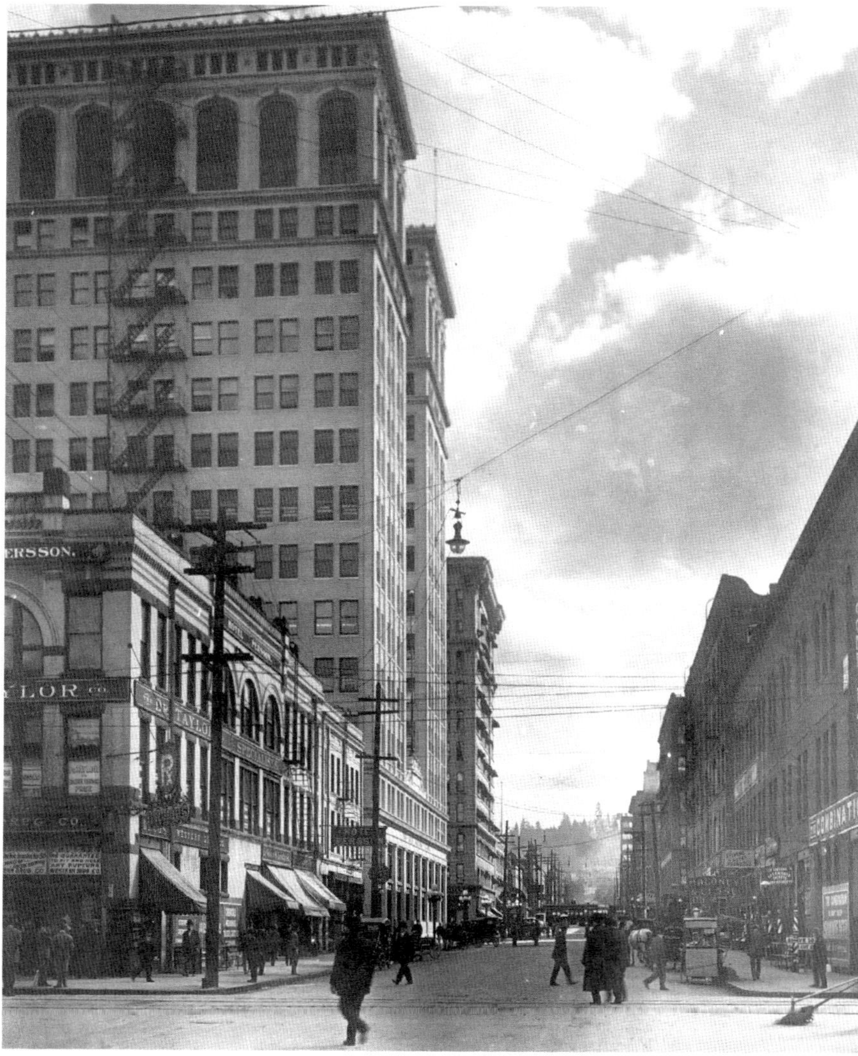

Stevens Street served as an important place of business through 1910. This photo even caught the piles of manure and the street sweeper's shovel. *Courtesy of the Ned M. Barnes Northwest Room, Spokane Public Library.*

had just begun the morning session. After lunching at the Spokane Hotel, they were planning to return to elect officers and create plans for action.

They carefully went through the process of adopting a constitution and bylaws. The state was to be divided into two sections. The east side would include all territory east of the Cascade Mountains. Each half of the organization would be supervised by its own set of officers.

For May, the highlight of the day was when the group voted her in as president. She had nominated a longtime friend of hers—a Washington State senator, R.A. Hutchinson—to be president, but he pulled out at the last minute. His decision opened the door for her to be elected, and she happily accepted the office when it was offered. Being elected president of the Washington Political Equality League was the vindication that she had been wishing for since July. And though she had not sat around feeling sorry for herself until October, the thought that her "home women" had seen her value and elected her president would be an encouragement to her for the rest of her life.[41]

28

CLUB WOMEN AND AGGRESSIVE ACTION

A few weeks later, Hutton congratulated herself on her decision to stop the open-air suffrage meetings, which she did when she saw the nation's labor unrest unfolding in Spokane. The International Workers of the World (IWW) were criticizing corrupt employment practices of local hiring agencies and making speeches about the issue on the city streets. They were finding supporters of their cause among unemployed miners who congregated in Spokane during the wintertime.

In August, May noticed the city had passed an ordinance against street speaking. But the unrest continued. On October 25, 1909, an IWW organizer was arrested for speaking on Stevens Street. He was jailed and then tried the next day.

Although May did not attend the trial, she followed it closely in the newspaper. She noted with interest that a judge had ruled the new street-speaking ordinance unconstitutional and had dismissed the charges against the organizer. The city was still hesitant, she noticed, because the judge had left an earlier ordinance against street speaking in place. Then he told the police that a better way to prosecute labor activists who spoke on the streets was to charge them with disorderly conduct.

Two days later, on October 29, May learned that her friend and fellow suffragist David Coates had convened a meeting with local socialists to discuss their position on the controversy. The group appointed a committee on free speech, which announced that they would join the IWW in the fight, scheduled to begin on November 2. Trying to offer moderation, the

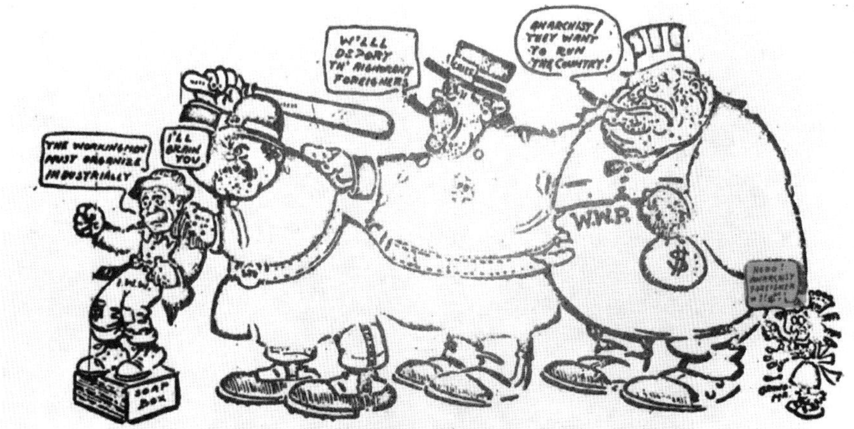

The Masters Do Not Want the Workers to Organise Industrially.

This cartoon describes the political power in Spokane of 1910. *Courtesy of the* Industrial Worker, *February 12, 1910, www.marxist.org.*

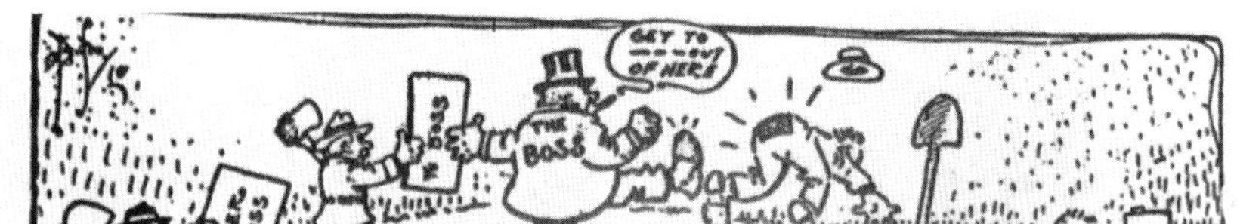

THE ENDLESS CHAIN—EMPLOYMENT SHARK, THE TRANSPORTATION AGENT AND THE BOSS—FLEECE THE WORKERS.

This cartoon illustrates miners getting squeezed between employment agencies and the mine owners. *Courtesy of the* Industrial Worker, *www.marxist.org.*

group agreed to stay out of the controversy if the courts freed the jailed labor activists and if local labor unions were again allowed to speak on the streets as the Salvation Army could. But when the city failed to respond, the socialists called for "all lovers of free speech" to come to town and join the street meetings. They intended to defy the street-speaking ordinance but still to maintain order at all meetings.

This moderation made it easier for May to maintain her friendship with Coates, but she still believed the labor activists were too aggressive. She congratulated herself on deciding to stop the open-air suffrage meetings in the parks. They seemed too much like the labor meetings on the street.

But not all of the suffragists shared May's worries. Sadie Coates, David's wife, and Sarah E. Commerford, president of the College Equal Suffrage Club, who had helped Baker with the park meetings, were both on hand to watch local court proceedings in November 1909. When the judge had overturned Spokane's most recent street-speaking ordinance, the ladies had joined other IWW supporters in applauding the decision. A *Chronicle* reporter noticed the suffragists' support for labor and duly reported their position in the newspaper.

Hutton was unhappy to see the suffragists so openly involved in the street-speaking trial. She watched the storm brewing in Spokane with mixed emotions. Her view from the fourth floor of the Hutton Building on the corner of Washington Street and Sprague allowed her to watch the unrest in the streets below without leaving the building.

May's anger over the way labor activists had been treated in North Idaho; her frustration when her own husband, a train engineer, had been thrown into a bullpen with striking miners; and her subsequent status change as a mine owner herself meant that the fight on the streets of Spokane pulled at her emotions in many ways. Her longtime sympathy for working class women and their children told her she should get involved, but she hesitated.

Then, in early December, Hutton noticed that the charismatic labor activist Elizabeth Gurley Flynn had been arrested in Spokane. The next day, she read in the *Spokane Press* that a pale and haggard Flynn had told a judge that she had been given the "third degree" by Police Chief Sullivan and two detectives. And when she had asked for her attorney to represent her, she had been denied.

May had connections to Flynn's attorney, Fred H. Moore, a local socialist and a friend of David C. Coates. Moreover, she knew his wife, Rose Moore, who was a suffragist and a member of the Woman's Club. The young couple helped bail Flynn out of jail, and they later may have introduced the activist to Hutton.

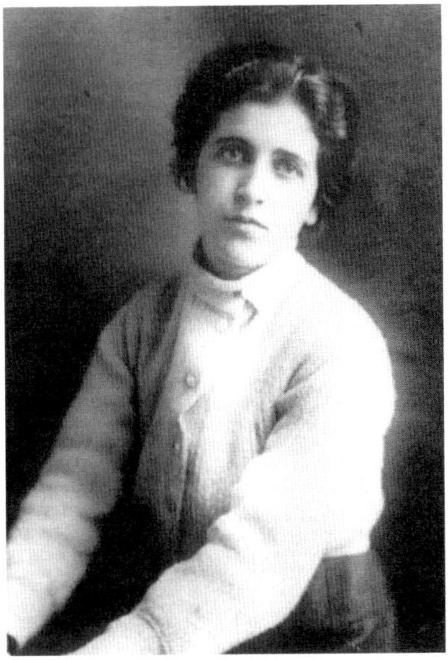

This photo of Elizabeth Gurley Flynn was taken a few years after her trial. *Courtesy of the Eastern Washington State Historical Society: Museum of Arts and Culture.*

Flynn, who was nineteen years old and several months pregnant, reminded May of the young women whom she had taken under her wing from the local Florence Crittenton Mission. Many others thought Flynn was a contradiction in femininity. Mrs. J.A. Jones—at least that was what local authorities called the activist—had intense blue eyes and black hair. On one hand, she looked like a respectable young married woman who was expecting her first child. On the other hand, the spellbinding Elizabeth Gurley Flynn could rally crowds of laborers.

May saw that Flynn had been released on bail and was telling about her experiences in the local jail. When the activist hinted that the police were encouraging male prisoners to have sexual relationships with the women inmates, May was alarmed. For example, Flynn said that one of her cellmates had been let out to go visit "Jake" during the night. Hutton decided it was time to act.

She knew that the decade-long quest for a police matron in Spokane had won a part-time matron who kept a full-time job elsewhere and was at the jail only when summoned by police officers or the sheriff. That arrangement could leave the incarcerated women in a man's environment for days without a woman there to intervene if other inmates or the jailers behaved inappropriately. She knew the only way to solve this problem was to introduce resident police matrons into the local jails.

She wanted to launch the fight to appoint a resident police matron for the jails but knew she had to do it carefully. She decided that the local women's club would be the best place to start. So, on December 6, she introduced a resolution for a resident police matron for the city jail. The club responded by establishing a four-person committee to see what could be done about it.

29

A STAIN ON THE GOOD NAME OF SPOKANE

The Woman's Club police matron committee was upstaged very soon. On November 8, only two days after Hutton made the proposal, Flynn was tried for conspiracy to incite a violation of the laws of Spokane. Several well-dressed women attended her trial, and two—both members of the Woman's Club—were slated to testify.

Ethel Stalford, daughter in-law of the socialist Emma Stalford, was one of them. Ethel testified that she had heard Flynn speak and that she had found nothing wrong in what she said. The young woman was third vice president and chair of the publicity committee of the Woman's Club. Laura House, the president of the Woman's Club and a bondholder for Flynn, was scheduled to testify on Flynn's behalf, but when the court found that she had not heard Flynn speak, she was not called to the stand.

A jury of six businessmen debated for twenty minutes and sentenced Flynn to three months in jail. Flynn's attorney, Fred Moore, renewed her bail and appealed to the Washington Supreme Court. Flynn's next trial was scheduled for February.

In the interim, Flynn made the rounds of local service clubs. She even spent some time outside the city, speaking in nearby towns. While she was gone, Ethel Stalford kept her message about Spokane's police department alive.

In the following two months, the discussion about adding a resident police matron made for daily news. On the morning of Sunday, January 9, the *Spokesman-Review* announced that Mayor Nelson Pratt favored

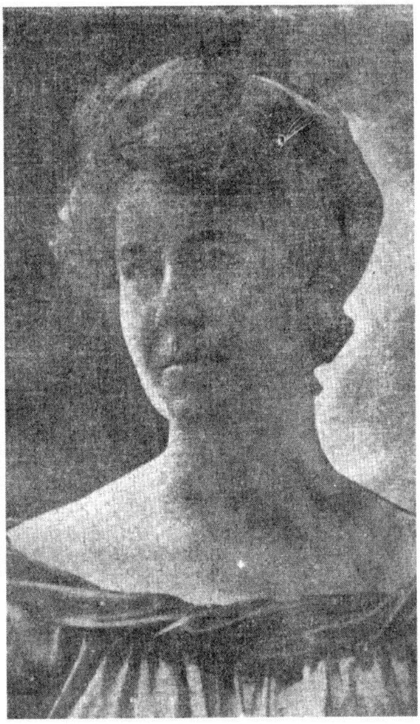

Ethel Stalford chaired the Woman's Club's Police Matron Committee. *Courtesy of the Eastern Washington State Historical Society: Museum of Arts and Culture.*

adding a police matron to the local jail staff, but that acting police chief John K. Sullivan argued that there was no need to increase women's presence in the jails. The current system of an on-call matron was sufficient, he proclaimed, adding that there was no room in the city jail for resident matrons.

Willing to be more reasonable, the sheriff simply agreed that Spokane County needed a resident jail matron. But his problem with fulfilling the need was similar to the city's. There simply was no room in the county jail to accommodate matrons. Moreover, additional expenses would be involved. Having a matron in the jail at all times would require hiring three women. Each would cover an eight-hour shift. And since there were two jails, the city and county would each have to hire three women.

Individual members of the Woman's Club began talking to reporters. Ethel Stalford asserted that women in local jails deserved the same respect that women outside jails received. Just because they had made bad choices did not mean they should be treated poorly. She noted that most cities with populations of 100,000 or more had jail matrons, among them both Seattle and Portland. She concluded, "Spokane is behind."[42]

The police matron campaign spread to other women's groups. The YWCA wanted to do the matron work for $95 per month. Thinking that their plan would allow them to have more say in who was appointed, the Woman's Club representatives suggested that the matron be selected by the city council instead.

Through the months that followed, city council members went back and forth. After voting once in January to appoint a resident matron, the council placed the matter on file after consulting with Chief Sullivan two weeks later. Sullivan countered that he would raise the current part-time matron's salary from $15 to $25 each month and then asked for the city to add $120 to its monthly appropriation for the department.

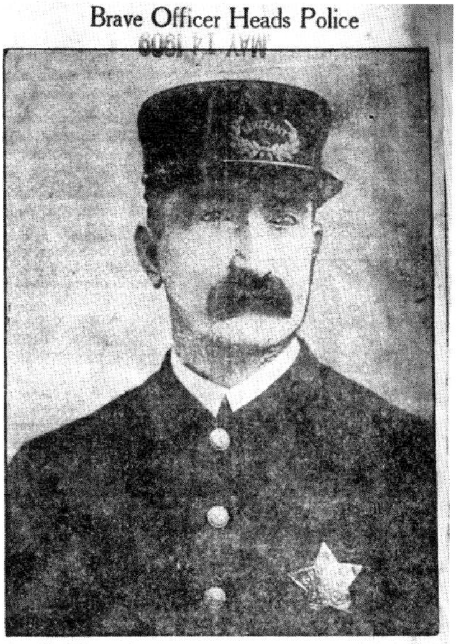

John T. Sullivan, acting police chief, had difficult choices to make and little experience to guide him through the free speech fight. *Courtesy of the Eastern Washington State Historical Society: Museum of Arts and Culture.*

Also in January, Blanche Mason, the assistant state labor commissioner from Olympia, toured the city jail and declared it bad for female prisoners. She found "trashy novels" and "half consumed" cigarettes on the floor. Young girls should not even be held there, she concluded, noting that only a woman police officer would be able to right the wrongs she found, as men would be entirely unfit to do so.[43]

Chief Sullivan sullenly responded, telling a reporter that he did not take Mason's suggestions seriously. He went on defiantly, "We don't intend to take advice about the department from women, either."[44] By early February, the chief had decided to put more money into his fight. He asked the city council to pay the part-time matron forty dollars per month.

The women responded by enlisting more supporters. The Woman's Club economic department members, headed by Mrs. Z.W. Commerford, visited a committee of the chamber of commerce in the Hutton Building. They came out jubilant, with the news that the chamber would support them. Likewise, by mid-February, they had the support of the city's graduate nurses and of members of the Elks lodge.

Woman's Club members decided to ramp up their campaign for resident matrons one evening at a banquet, during which La Reine Baker told them they were too easily put off by promises from the city council and urged them to use aggressive action. The ladies listened and decided to act. They put together a plan to storm the city council on the following day and selected Ethel Stalford and Baker to lead the group.

In late February, twenty-four women—along with several of their husbands, including Hutton, Commerford and House—appeared at city hall. When council members gave their attention to the group, Ethel quickly went forward. She charged that conditions in the city jail were "a stain on the good name of Spokane." Seventy-five minutes later, after discussing outrageous conditions in the cells and hinting that the police bribed council members not to appoint police matrons, she asked why, if so many voters in Spokane wanted matrons appointed, the council would not give them what they asked for.

Council members responded first by suggesting that a committee be selected to conduct a probe into the conditions at the city jail. Stalford quickly responded that that would not be necessary; instead, she and her cohorts simply wanted three police matrons appointed. It was the right thing to do.

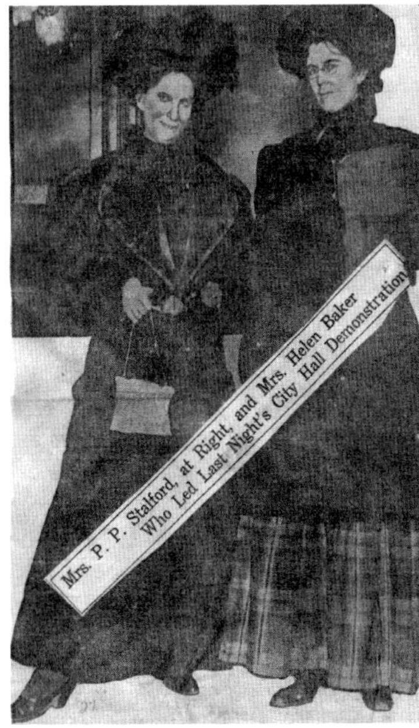

La Reine Baker and Ethel Stalford posed just before they led the "storm" on city hall. *Courtesy of the Eastern Washington State Historical Society: Museum of Arts and Culture.*

Before the club women left, the council had passed a resolution to hire three matrons and pay them seventy-five dollars each per month. The women were so excited that it was several minutes after the resolution had been approved before people in the council room could hear themselves. Ethyl threw one more barb out before the women left. She offered the sincere hope that the council would have the courage of conviction and the sense to avoid another of their famous reversals. The preservation of Spokane's fair name required that they do something.

30
STANDING PAT

The honor of the police department and its employees was an important secondary theme in the second trial of Elizabeth Gurley Flynn in Spokane's Superior Court, which began on February 9. A detective and police captain, Martin J. Burns, served as assistant prosecutor and witness in the trial. He had been the police officer who arrested Flynn, and he had helped Sullivan and Pugh interview the activist before they sent her to the county jail.

Flynn and a local labor leader, Charlie Filigno, were charged with conspiracy. Fred Moore, along with an attorney from Chicago, headed up the defense. Fred C. Pugh, a feisty man who had little patience for labor activists, oversaw the prosecution team. He raised his voice frequently enough during the trial that local papers said he was "thundering." His loose talk outside the courtroom gave ammunition to the defense lawyers.

IWW supporters and curious onlookers packed the courtroom. Twelve local women, including Commerford and Moore, occupied reserved seats inside the wooden railing. Flynn, dressed in a bright red one-piece suit with a white collar and a gray scarf, sat quietly at first, smiling occasionally. When Moore asked her to tell the jury what she had said in Spokane, the question brought out her talent. She got a fire in her eyes and color in her cheeks, and her earnest, conversational tone—directed to the jury—captivated the entire courtroom. She spoke so easily that Pugh interrupted her once to verify that she was sticking to her topic. When she was done, the onlookers in the courtroom sat quietly for a

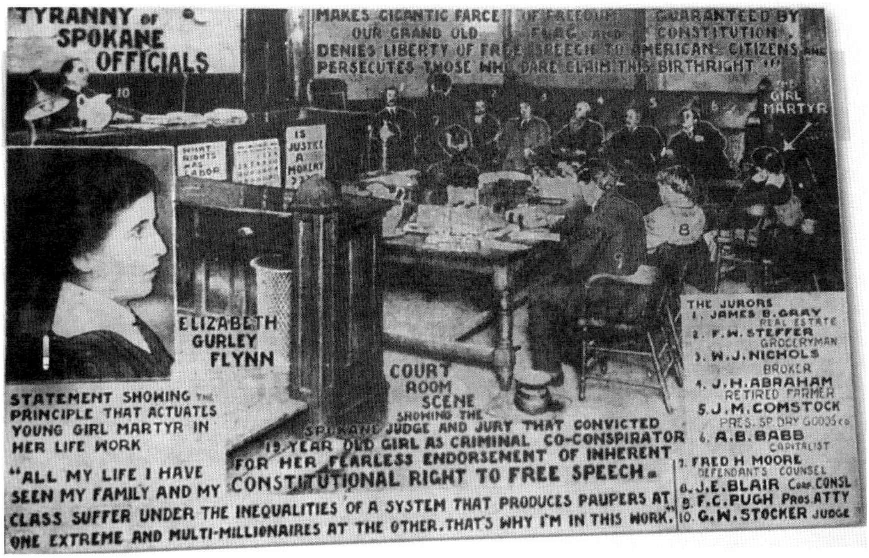

This postcard gives a glimpse inside the courtroom during Flynn and Filigno's trial. *Courtesy of Duane Broyles.*

moment. Even Pugh complimented her because she had remained true to herself.

Flynn's talk won the jury to her side—but not to her cause. After deliberating for seventeen hours, they acquitted her but convicted Filigno. Prosecutor Pugh and Flynn were both incensed by the decision. Flynn was irritated that her codefendant had been sentenced to four months in jail.

Pugh, in his usual fiery style, confronted the foreman of the jury in the lobby. He asked why they had acquitted the guiltiest and convicted the least guilty. The man replied, "She ain't a criminal, Fred, an' you know it! If you think this jury, or any jury, is goin' to send that pretty Irish girl to jail merely for being big-hearted and idealistic, to mix with all those crooks down at the pen, you've got another guess comin.'"[45]

Flynn's trial closed just as the news of the ladies' "storm" on the city council broke. Stalford had insisted that she could document that conditions in the city jail were vicious, even though Flynn had spent the night in the county jail. Chief Sullivan angrily responded that the jailers had been slandered. He promised to prove that her facts were wrong. Furthermore, he suggested that the policemen who supervised the city jail should sue Stalford. He called for a committee of business *men* to be appointed to investigate conditions in the city jail.

Stalford stood by what she had said. Moreover, she reminded anyone who would listen that club women had been asking for a police matron long before the IWW controversy hit Spokane. It was absurd, she said, that they had to go to the city council to ask for decency and cleanliness.

May Hutton took a public stand for Stalford soon after the storm on city hall. She reiterated the need for a resident police matron. She also backed Ethel while many other club women began falling away.

Despite her earlier push for aggressive action, when La Reine Baker heard that Sullivan was talking about lawsuits, she quickly separated herself from Ethel. So intent on making a break with her, she gave a written statement to a reporter describing Ethel's accusations as a disgrace. She said that talking that way hurt the work of the Woman's Club and charged that Stalford had learned to speak so aggressively because she sympathized with Flynn and the IWW.

Others began pulling back their support for a resident matron. The pastor of Grace Methodist Church went to city hall to take his name off the petition asking for a matron. He explained that he still supported the idea but wanted nothing to do with accusing the current police department.

On February 25, the executive committee of the Woman's Club met privately to discuss the situation. They chose to stand fully behind Ethel Stalford. The chair of the Police Matron Committee, she had been authorized to speak for the club. In contrast, La Reine Baker had no official backing to speak for the club.

By February 27, local papers were talking about factions within the club itself. Some society women were going to the city council and offering their

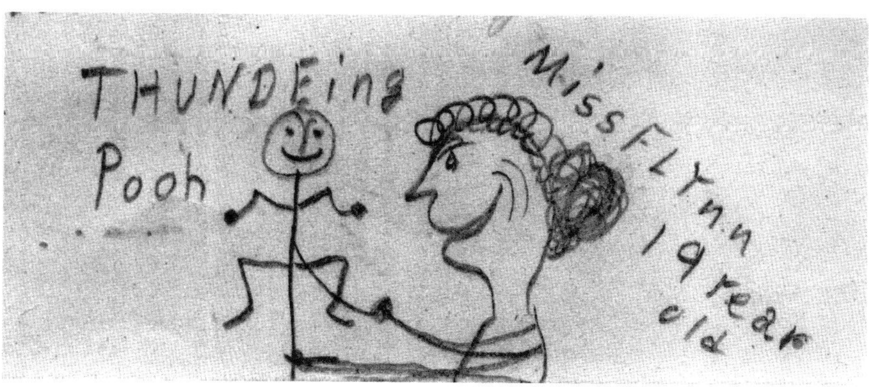

An anonymous artist sent this cartoon to prosecuting attorney Fred Pugh. *Courtesy of the Washington State Archives, Eastern Regional Branch, Cheney, Washington.*

services as volunteer matrons. Others said they were worried that Ethel would not be able to prove her accusations. Still others argued that La Reine's comments were out of line and she should be asked to resign.

Club president Laura House sent an official statement to the *Chronicle*, which was published on February 28. She asserted that she had been compelled to do so by the quantity of misinformation that was circulating through the town. There were no factions in the club, she said, and they planned to ask no members to resign. Furthermore, the Social Economics Department would hold a meeting on March 8, at which time they would get a full report from the Police Matron Committee. She concluded by reemphasizing the club's commitment to seeing that resident police matrons were appointed.

In March, while IWW leaders negotiated with the city to end the free speech fight, the Woman's Club members worked to establish more normal patterns of activity. At the first semi-monthly meeting, House reported that city council members would give their resident police matron request another

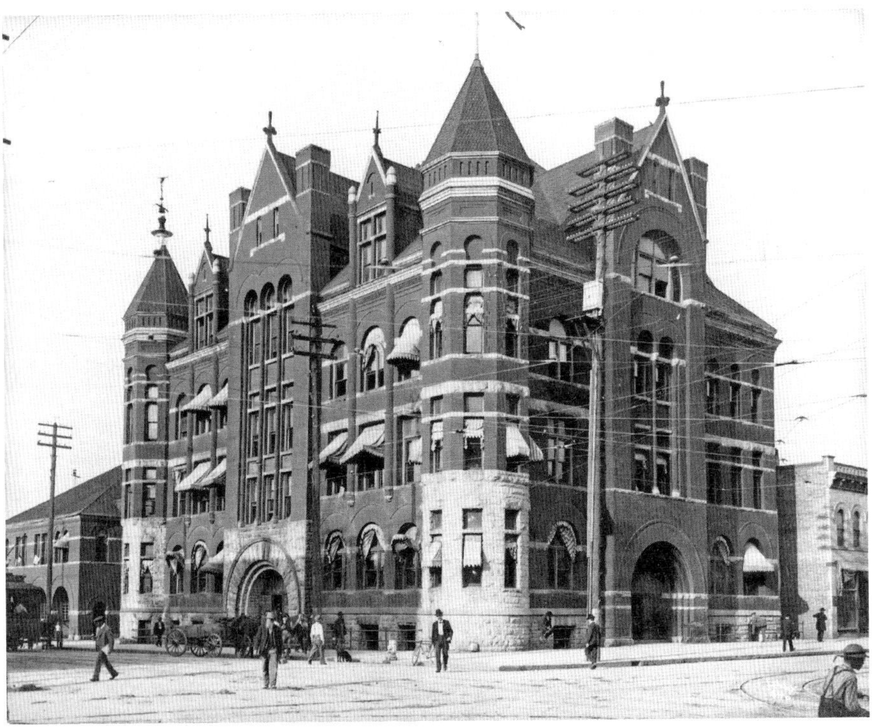

This building served as Spokane's city hall between the Fire of 1889 and 1912. *Courtesy of Ned M. Barnes Northwest Room, Spokane Public Library.*

hearing on Tuesday, March 8. The club decided they wanted to continue pushing for a resident police matron and selected Laura to represent them at the council meeting.

House attended the meeting, and the city council duly passed a resolution to hire three resident matrons for Spokane's jail, only to be met with opposition from Chief Sullivan once again. The chief argued that hiring a resident matron was unnecessary at that time. In addition, he insisted that the Salvation Army "lassie" was doing a fine job on the salary of forty dollars per month. Instead of hiring a matron, the council decided to establish a committee to investigate conditions in the jail. They would not decide to appoint resident matrons unless the committee found the conditions in the jail were bad. Everyone was standing pat.

31

THE FIGHT FOR POLICE MATRON IS HISTORY

The Woman's Club complained that city council was conducting an investigation when it should have simply decided to do the right thing and hired a matron. But the ladies went along with the committee idea, nominating Dr. George McDowell to represent the Woman's Club. He had made a name for himself as a top-notch surgeon and was recognized as a leader in reform, having served as a longtime board member of the Florence Crittenton Mission.

Another surgeon on the team, Dr. T.L. Catterson, was appointed by city council. He chaired the committee and held its meetings in his offices. With far less interest in women's concerns, he chafed when the ladies insisted that they offer the people they interviewed legal immunity, replying, "Of course we will do that."

The third committee member was James W. Kramer, a Baptist minister. Shortly after being appointed, Dr. McDowell resigned from the committee, insisting that he would not help to whitewash the police department. Reverend Kramer stayed on, willing to compromise with Catterson about how to conduct meetings.

Spokane's activists were not happy with the committee. Club women joined with labor leaders and other residents of the city. Their cooperation, which had been growing over the last year, began to show in political power in March 1910. Representatives of these groups—the women's clubs, labor unions and German societies—met and voted to push city council for better representation on the jail probe committee.

They requested that the jail investigation be conducted in closed meetings. Members of the groups also refused to give interviews to the committee unless their requests were granted.

Mayor Pratt testily responded that the probe committee was his, not theirs. Nevertheless, he asked the committee to appoint representatives of club women, German societies and labor interests. Then, city leaders threw D.C. Coates out after he led a large march to city hall and attempted to speak to council members.

The committee worked diligently and soon announced an investigation plan. By mid-March, members still had not found anyone who accused the police of wrongdoing. So, they began interviewing people who had previous experience working with the police department, including a few people who had moved on to other jobs. When that was done, they found former inmates to interview.

One was a twenty-nine-year-old woman who went by the name of Stella Brown. Charged with blackmail, she had been incarcerated for a few hours and said she had not been mistreated by anyone while she was there. Stella thought they had left her alone because she had such a fiery temper. Before she finished the interview, she said she had heard other women complaining about being mistreated in jail. When the committee pushed for more information, she refused to talk, saying she was afraid she would get in trouble.

Maggie Cunningham, a German immigrant, had been arrested twice: once for vagrancy and a second time for running a disorderly house. Insisting that she had not been mistreated by police, she focused her complaints on a madam who persecuted the girls she disliked by sending them to jail. When asked, Cunningham said she saw no reason why any girl would not want to do an interview like the one she was doing.

The committee interviewed fifteen women who were former inmates or had in some other way ended up on the wrong side of the law. They interviewed seven police workers, including two detectives, John Sullivan, the Salvation Army police matron and Dr. Mary Latham. In addition, they interviewed a former jailer, a nurse and an IWW activist who had been an inmate but was now a member of the committee.

In addition to conducting the interviews, committee members visited the city jail at bedtime, watching as the inmates went to their cells to retire for the night. Sullivan, anxious to clear the jailers' reputations, had adopted an open policy, so anyone who wanted to visit the jail could do so, with a jailer supervising.

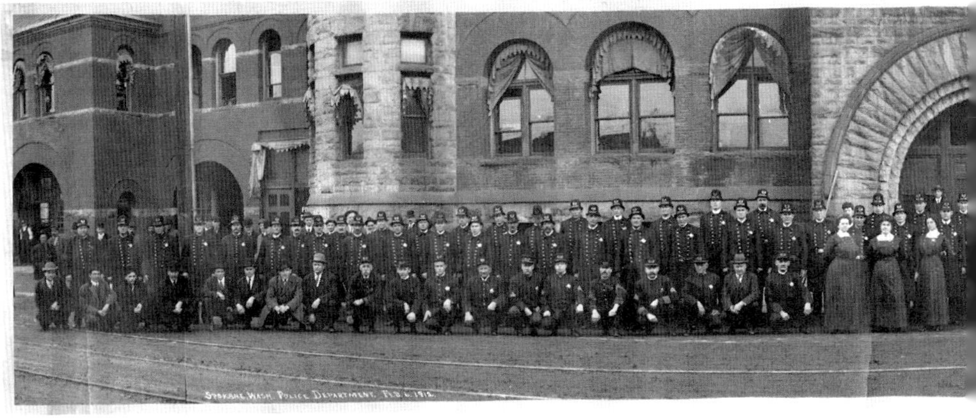

Inez Delashmutt, one of the club women who had offered her services as a volunteer matron and a member of the investigative committee, made a statement that was included in the final report. She had by chance met Sarah Commerford on the street one day and asked her what she knew about the women who claimed they had been mistreated in the jail. The younger woman vaguely answered that there were a lot of affidavits that Mrs. Moore, Mrs. Stalford or maybe Mrs. House had. Then she brightened up and suggested that Delashmutt go interview the president of the YWCA, because "she knows a lot about the trouble with the police force."[46]

Inez visited the YWCA to find out whether the organization had any further information about the treatment of women in the city jail. She was immediately told, "Your information is wrong." The YWCA leader insisted that she simply did not deal with the type of women who stayed in jail overnight. The jailers sent her teens who had committed only small offenses. She did what she could for the girls, then sent them to the Little Girls' Christian Association. Inez left thinking that the club women who had been the most outspoken about outrages in the police department knew very little about the situation.

Ethel Stalford did not back down. She wrote letters to both Mayor Pratt and Chief Sullivan in which she lauded the Woman's Club. It existed, she said, to educate and socialize. If the ladies could use the group to teach the residents of Spokane how to be better citizens, the club should be respected. Then she answered the specific charges against herself. She was not Flynn's bond holder—her mother-in-law, Emma, was. And she had testified under oath in court that she was not a member of the IWW. Finally, she had made no specific charges against Sullivan or the men who worked under him.

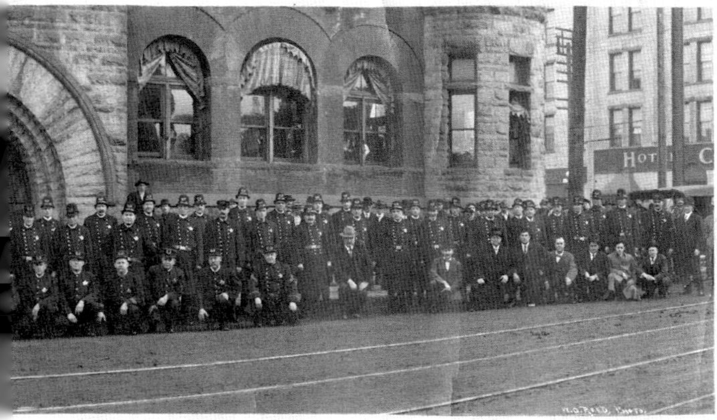

This 1912 photo of the Spokane Police Department shows the context within which police matrons worked. *Courtesy of the Eastern Washington State Regional Archives: Museum of Arts and Culture.*

The committee made their final report to the city council in May. They concluded that the club women had not sufficiently documented their charges. Stalford and her associates had finally submitted affidavits, but the committee had been able to contact only one woman who had signed them. And regarding the charges that the jail was full of "vermin," the committee said the facility was "tolerably clean."

They did assert that the women's bathroom needed a blanket hung over its open doorway and recommended that female inmates be issued clean bedding when they arrived. In the end, they sided with the club women, concluding that "common decency" required the police to hire resident matrons. But they also gave Sullivan a nod by saying that appointing a matron could wait until new facilities had been built.

"Longstanding Fight for Police Matron Now Is History" a headline in the *Chronicle* read on May 30. The article explained that three women, not the choices the club women had presented, had agreed on that day to become Spokane's first resident police matrons. They were Captain Bertha Smith, the formerly part-time matron from the Salvation Army; Mrs. N.W. Allender of the Volunteers of America; and a widow, Mrs. Ella Jones, of the Universalist Church.

32

VOTING AT LAST!

While the resident police matrons were adjusting to using the same small space that the female inmates had to live in, local club women and suffragists were resuming more normal routines. The women in jail were receiving the care and respect they deserved, so the club women moved on.

In late 1909, Hutton had established the headquarters for the Washington Political Equality League next to her apartments on the fourth floor of the Hutton Building. Her husband, Levi, had donated the space to the group for a year while they were wrapping up the suffrage campaign for Washington. Now the league had its doors open full time, with a knowledgeable employee there to help answer questions and distribute publicity materials and other resources. With the suffrage office located literally next door to her home, May could drop in at any time to keep abreast of what was happening and help when needed.

May frequently had speaking appointments around Spokane. In February, she joined David C. Coates and made a presentation on suffrage to the local Socialist Party. The speeches were well received; the party voted to join the Woman's Club in their quest to add resident police matrons and pursue suffrage.

That spring, the Woman's Club voted to raise money for their own building. They elected May to chair the building committee. It was an honor—and a big job, too. It required fundraising as well as looking for property. This committee eventually settled on a location on the lower South Hill, at Ninth and Walnut.

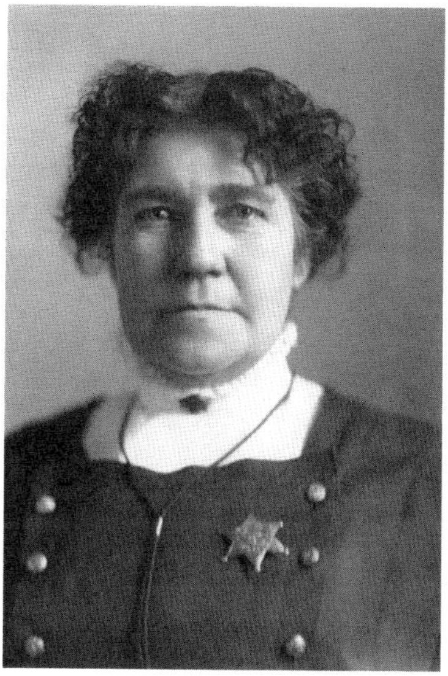

Ella Jones was one of the first resident police matrons. *Courtesy of the Eastern Washington State Regional Archives: Museum of Arts and Culture.*

May was also branching out into other activities. She had been recruiting other women to join her in establishing a school for young women who wanted to be housekeepers and cooks. In May 1910, she wrote a letter to John D. Rockefeller, asking him to donate money for the project, in hopes that he would build a school for them.

At about the same time, anonymous anti-suffragist brochures sent from Boston were showing up in mailboxes around Spokane. Hutton talked to the *Chronicle* about it. She told the reporter how difficult it had been, while promoting the proposed amendment for Washington, to find an anti-suffrage pamphlet sitting on every desk in Olympia. She had recently returned from a trip to Massachusetts. She thought it not too surprising that the pamphlets should come from there, because she thought the women there were self-centered.

In June, Hutton gave a reception in honor of Henrietta Crossman, the president of the Actresses Suffrage League, and niece of Rachel Foster Avery, the first vice president of NAWSA. She sent invitations to five hundred men and women and then published in the *Chronicle* a general invitation to anyone interested. The guests would also be treated to a talk by a member of the Woman's Club telling about their new Day Nursery, which was caring for twenty-eight little ones and charging only five cents a day.

While May was keeping busy with a myriad of jobs in Spokane, the younger suffragists were spreading their wings. La Reine Baker traveled in South Dakota, lecturing on women's right to vote. Ethel Stalford and Rose Moore put on their most charming manners and visited saloons in the city. They did so to assure the men there that they would not use the vote to close saloons, a tactic that worked so well the women went to several saloons. Sarah Commerford and Rose Moore helped organize suffrage clubs in nearby towns.

The women activists were all feeling positive. Certainly, there were still anti-suffragists around. Hutton read about one in a local paper and called

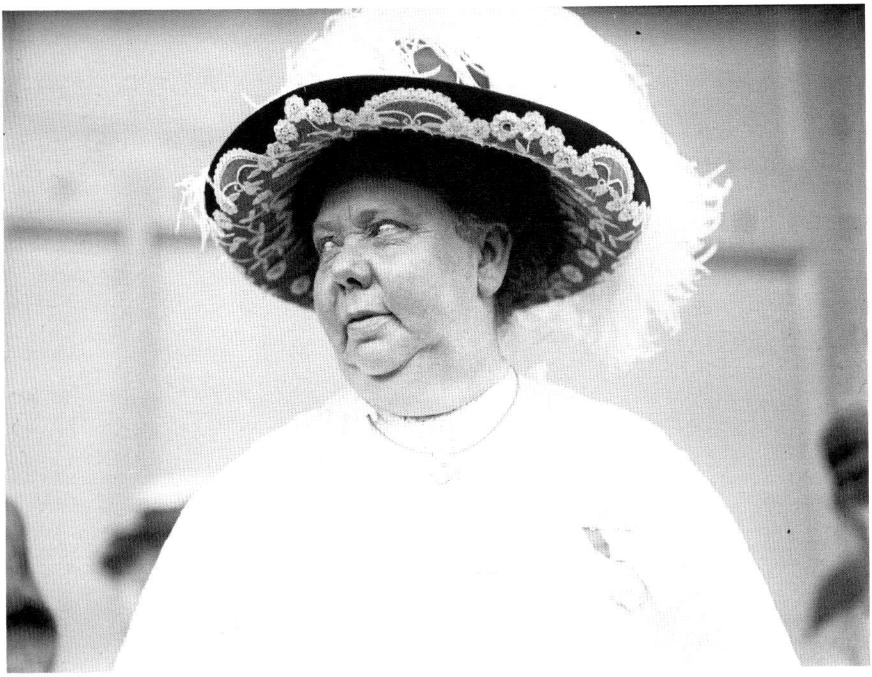

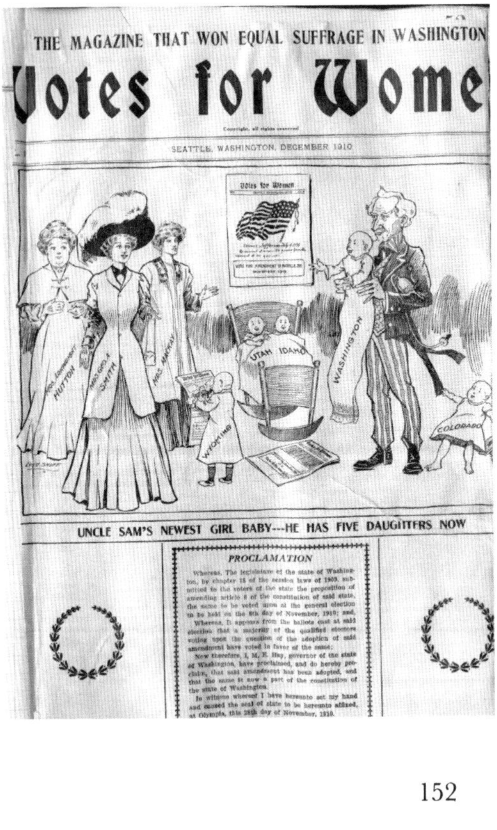

THE MAGAZINE THAT WON EQUAL SUFFRAGE IN WASHINGTON

Votes for Wome

SEATTLE, WASHINGTON, DECEMBER 1910

UNCLE SAM'S NEWEST GIRL BABY---HE HAS FIVE DAUGHTERS NOW

PROCLAMATION

Whereas, The legislature of the state of Washington, by chapter 18 of the session laws of 1909, submitted to the voters of the state the proposition of amending article 6 of the constitution of said state, the same to be voted upon at the general election to be held on the 8th day of November, 1910; and,

Whereas, It appears from the ballots cast at said election that a majority of the qualified electors voting upon the question of the adoption of said amendment have voted in favor of the same;

Now therefore, I, M. E. Hay, governor of the state of Washington, have proclaimed, and do hereby proclaim, that said amendment has been adopted, and that the same is now a part of the constitution of the state of Washington.

In witness whereof I have hereunto set my hand and caused the seal of state to be hereunto affixed, at Olympia, this 28th day of November, 1910.

Above: Hutton was a delegate to the Democratic National Convention in 1912. *Courtesy of the National Archives, www.archives.gov.*

Left: This 1910 cartoon, honoring suffrage states and Washington suffragists, was published in *Votes for Women*, the magazine that won for women the right to vote in Washington. *Courtesy of the Eastern Washington State Regional Archives: Museum of Arts and Culture.*

to talk to her. She congratulated the lady for standing up for her convictions, and the two ended their conversation on a positive note. May wrote to a friend that fall, telling her she was looking forward to seeing the voters in her state give women the vote. As election time approached, the feeling in the air was more buoyant than it ever had been before.

On November 9, 1910, May spent her day at the headquarters for the Washington Political Equality League. It was like a day-long party. Friends were dropping by in a steady stream to congratulate her, even before they heard the final vote count. May was the queen of the day in Spokane. And in the view of Spokane's suffragists, she deserved a large part of the credit for winning the vote for Washington women. Hutton could put another feather in her cap.

That day, male voters in Washington cast twenty-two thousand votes more for suffrage. The *Chronicle* headline announced, "Women Given the Vote." Washington had become the fifth state to give women the vote. May Arkwright Hutton could once again vote—now as a full citizen of the state of Washington.

NOTES

Chapter 4

1. "For the Friendless," *Review*, May 18, 1890, 5.

Chapter 5

2. "It Is a Noble Work," *Review*, September 7, 1890.

Chapter 6

3. "The County Sick," *Review*, April 3, 1891, 3.
4. "The County Poor," *Chronicle*, April 22, 1891, 5.

Chapter 7

5. "Christine the Waif," *Spokesman-Review*, June 14, 1891, 6:1.

Chapter 9

6. "Special Committee Reports," *Spokesman-Review*, February 3, 1897, 3.
7. "Were Hopping Mad," *Spokesman-Review*, February 5, 1897, 5.
8. "Home Scores Once," *Spokesman-Review*, February 17, 1897, 5.

Chapter 11

9. Kershner, *Carl Maxey*.

Chapter 12

10. Nevada M. Bloomer, V. John Todd, J.E. Gandy and H.A. Clarke, August 14, 1888.

Chapter 13

11. "Spokane County Woman Suffrage Association," *Northwest Tribune*, September 30, 1881, 3.

Chapter 14

12. "Women Who Think," *Spokane Daily Chronicle*, June 4, 1898, 5.
13. "Women of the West," *Spokane Daily Chronicle*, June 11, 1898, 8; "Brains, Beauty, Wit and Worth," *Spokane Daily Chronicle*, June 14, 1898, 5.

Chapter 16

14. "She Hopes to Vote," *Spokane Daily Chronicle*, August 26, 1898, 7.

Chapter 17

15. "Mean Trick by Suffragists," *Spokane Daily Chronicle*, October 17, 1898, 7.
16. "Want Women to Vote," *Spokane Daily Chronicle*, October 24, 1898, 3.
17. "Women on the Warpath," *Spokane Daily Chronicle*, November 3, 1898, 7.

Chapter 18

18. "Suffrage Gain," *Spokane Daily Chronicle*, December 8, 1898, 8.
19. Ibid.

Chapter 19

20. "60 Years Ago," *Spokane Daily Chronicle*, November 14, 1962, 4.
21. "Fail to Form a Rescue League," *Spokesman-Review*, February 29, 1904, 4.

Chapter 21

22. "Ask Voters to Give Women the Ballot," *Spokane Daily Chronicle*, February 20, 1908, 9.
23. Newspaper clipping, Scrapbook 3, 10. May Arkwright Hutton Collection, MSSC 55, Northwest Museum of Arts and Culture/Eastern Washington State Historical Society, Spokane, Washington.

Chapter 22

24. Grace Roffey Pratt, "The Great-Hearted Huttons of the Coeur d'Alenes," *Montana Magazine* (April 1967): 20–33, xvii, 1/1, May Arkwright Hutton Papers, MSSC 55, Northwest Museum of Arts and Culture/Eastern Washington State Historical Society, Spokane, Washington.
25. Hutton Speech, November 1908, 1/2, May Arkwright Hutton Papers, MSSC 55, Northwest Museum of Arts and Culture/Eastern Washington State Historical Society, Spokane, Washington.

26. Letter to Dr. Eaton, November 5, 1908, 1/2, May Arkwright Hutton Papers, MSSC 55, Northwest Museum of Arts and Culture/Eastern Washington State Historical Society, Spokane, Washington.
27. Letter to Emma Smith Devoe, November 21, 1908, 1/3, May Arkwright Hutton Papers, MSSC 55, Northwest Museum of Arts and Culture/ Eastern Washington State Historical Society, Spokane, Washington.

Chapter 23

28. Ross-Nazzal, *Winning the West for Women*, 127.
29. "Women May Soon Vote," *Spokane Daily Chronicle*, February 23, 1909, 1.

Chapter 24

30. Letter to La Reine Baker, April 7, 1909, 1/5, May Arkwright Hutton Papers, MSSC 55, Northwest Museum of Arts and Culture/Eastern Washington State Historical Society, Museum of Arts and Culture, Spokane, Washington.
31. Letter to La Reine Baker, May 6, 1909, 1/5, May Arkwright Hutton Papers MSSC 55, Eastern Washington State Historical Society, Museum of Arts and Culture, Spokane, Washington.
32. Letter to Harriet Taylor Upton, May 6, 1909, 1/5, May Arkwright Hutton Papers, MSSC 55, Northwest Museum of Arts and Culture/ Eastern Washington State Historical Society, Museum of Arts and Culture, Spokane, Washington.

Chapter 25

33. "Lock 'Em In," *Spokane Daily Chronicle*, July 2, 1909, 1.
34. Stevenson, *Women's Votes, Women's Voices*, 48–49.
35. "Hanged Herself," *Spokane Daily Chronicle*, July 10, 1909, 1–2.

Chapter 26

36. "Suffragists Camp," *Ottawa Citizen*, July 26, 1909.
37. "Speak at Coeur d'Alene Park," *Spokesman-Review*, July 30, 1909, 15.

38. Letter to Mrs. Homer Hill, August 13, 1909, 1/8, May Arkwright Hutton Papers, MSSC 55, Northwest Museum of Arts and Culture/Eastern Washington State Historical Society, Spokane, Washington.
39. Letter to Mrs. Leonia Brown, September 23, 1909, 1/9, May Arkwright Hutton Papers, MSSC 55, Northwest Museum of Arts and Culture/ Eastern Washington State Historical Society, Spokane, Washington.
40. Letter to Abigail Scott Duniway, August 13, 1909, 1/9, May Arkwright Hutton Papers, MSSC 55, Northwest Museum of Arts and Culture/ Eastern Washington State Historical Society, Spokane, Washington.

Chapter 27

41. Letter to Harriet Taylor Upton, October 18, 1909, 1/9, May Arkwright Hutton Papers, MSSC 55, Northwest Museum of Arts and Culture/ Eastern Washington State Historical, Spokane, Washington.

Chapter 29

42. "Club Women Urge Need of Matron," *Spokesman-Review*, January 10, 1910, 4, 7.
43. "Says Spokane Jail Debases Women," *Spokesman-Review*, January 17, 1910, 1, 6.
44. "Scouts Woman 'Cop' Idea," January 17, 1910, Police Scrapbooks, 278, EWSHS.

Chapter 30

45. Dubofsky, *We Shall Be All*, 103.

Chapter 31

46. Sullivan Report, Inquiry into the Police Department, 1910, Washington State Archives, Eastern Regional Branch, Cheney, WA.

BIBLIOGRAPHY

Public Records

Spokane Public Library

Censuses, U.S., 1900 and 1910
Photographs
Sanborn Maps
Spokane City Directories, R.L. Polk & Company, 1883–1910

Washington State Archives, Central Regional Branch

Gladys Isham v. City of Spokane, case file #27482, 1940

Washington State Archives, Eastern Regional Branch, Cheney, Washington

Auditing Committee Record (City)

Letter to Fred Pugh In the Matter of the Investigation of the Police Department of the City of Spokane by a Committee Consisting of Dr. Thomas Catterson and Others
Spokane City Council Minutes
Spokane County Clerk
Spokane County Commissioners Records

Washington State Archives, Olympia

Governor's Correspondence
Journal of the House
Journal of the Senate
Pierce County Birth and Death Records
Suffrage Papers

Newspapers and Periodicals

Inland Herald
Northwest Temperance Advocate
Northwest Tribune
Seattle Post-Intelligencer
Seattle Times
Spokane Daily Chronicle
Spokane Times
Spokesman-Review
Union Signal

Primary Documents

Papers

Charles Mackin, Papers
James Rebmann, SJ, Papers

Jesuit Oregon Archives, Gonzaga University, Spokane
Joseph Cataldo, SJ, Papers

Northwest Museum of Arts and Culture: Eastern Washington State Historical Society, Spokane

Anna Stratton Diary
Charlotte Pinkham Hamblen Diary
Ladies' Benevolent Society Minutes
May Arkwright Hutton Papers
Photograph Collection
Spokane Police Department Scrapbooks
Woman's Christian Temperance Union Papers

Saint Joseph's Family Center, Spokane

Sisters of St. Francis Scrapbooks

Providence Archives, Seattle

Chronicle of Sacred Heart Hospital
Mother Joseph Papers
Photograph collection

University of Washington, Seattle

Washington State Federation of Women's Clubs Papers

Washington State University, Holland Library

Elizabeth Tappan Tannett Papers

Spokane Woman's Club

Secretaries' Minutes, 1905–10

Theses and Dissertations

Engle, Nancy Driscol. "Benefitting a City, Women, Respectability and Reform, 1886–1910." PhD dissertation, University of Florida, 2003.

Farless, Patricia. "Gender Need Not Apply: The Impact of the Fourteenth Amendment of the United States." Master's thesis, University of Central Florida, 1996.

Knight, Johnathan David. "The Spokane Fresno Free Speech Fights of the International Workers of the World, 1909–1911." Master's thesis, Washington State University, 1991.

Rettmann, Jef. "Prostitution in Spokane." Master's thesis, Eastern Washington University, 1995.

PRIMARY BOOKS

Annual Report of the Board of Health of the City of Spokane Washington. N.p.: Shaw-Borden Company, 1894.

Croly, Mrs. J.C. *The History of the Woman's Club Movement in America.* New York: Henry G. Allen & Company, 1898.

Duniway, Abigail Scott. *Path Breaking: An Autobiographical History of the Equal Suffrage Movement in Pacific Coast States.* Portland, OR: James Kerns and Abbot Company, 1914.

Flynn, Elizabeth Gurley. *The Rebel Girl: An Autobiography.* Revised ed. New York: International Publishers, 1973.

Hook, Harry H., and Francis J. McGuire. *Spokane Falls Illustrated: The Metropolis of Eastern Washington.* Spokane, WA: Spokane Board of Trade, 1889.

SECONDARY SOURCES

Arnold, Howard S. *Spokane Police Department. 1879–1976.* Napa, CA: Walsworth Publishing, 1977.

Baker, La Reine Helen. *Race Improvement*. New York: Dodd Mead, 1912.

Bamonte, Suzanne, and Tony Bamonte. *Life Behind the Badge,* Spokane, WA: Tornado Creek Publications, 2008.

Blair, Karen J. *Women in the Pacific Northwest History*. Revised ed. Seattle: University of Washington Press, 2001.

Butler, Anne M. *Gendered Justice in the American West: Women Prisoners in Men's Penitentiaries*. Urbana: University of Illinois Press, 1995.

Camp, Helen. *Iron in Her Soul*. Pullman: Washington State University Press, 1995.

Cochran, Barbara F. *Seven Frontier Women and the Founding of Spokane Falls*. Spokane, WA: Tornado Creek Publications, 2011.

Dubofsky, Melvin. *We Shall Be All.* abridged. ed. Champaign: University of Illinois Press, 2000, 103.

Dubois, Ellen Carol. *Woman's Suffrage and Women's Rights*. New York: New York University Press, 1998.

Duda, John, ed. *Wanted: Men to Fill the Jails of Spokane: Fighting for Free Speech with the Hobo Agitators of the I.W.W.* Chicago: Charles H. Kerr Publishing Company, 2009.

Durham, Nelson W. *Spokane and the Inland Empire: Pictorial and Biographical*. Vols. 1 & 2. Chicago: S.J. Clarke Publishing Company, 1912.

Edwards, Jonathan, Rev. *An Illustrated History of Spokane County, State of Washington, 1847–1929*. N.p.: W.H. Lever Publisher, 1900.

Fahey, John. "The Nevada Bloomer Case." *Columbia Magazine* (Summer 1988): 42–45.

Fargo, Lucille F. "Mrs. Hercules." Unpublished manuscript, Ned M. Barnes Room, Spokane Public Library, n.d.

Fifty Golden Years: A Short History of Sacred Heart Hospital. Spokane, WA: Acme Stamp and Printing Company, 1936.

Ginzberg, Lori. *Women and the Work of Benevolence: Morality, Politics and Class in the Nineteenth Century America*. New Haven, CT: Yale University Press, 1990.

Haarsager, Sandra. *Organized Womanhood: Cultural Politics in the Pacific Northwest, 1840–1920*. Norman: University of Oklahoma Press, 1997.

Horner, Patricia Voeller. "May Arkwright Hutton: Suffragist and Politician." In *Women in Pacific Northwest History, An Anthology*, ed. Karen Blair. Seattle: University of Washington Press, 1988.

Hunt, Linda Lawrence. *Bold Spirit: Helga Estby's Forgotten Walk Across Victorian America*. Moscow: University of Idaho Press, 2003.

Kershner, Jim. *Carl Maxey: A Fighting Life*. Seattle: University of Washington Press, 2015.

Larson, T.A. "The Woman Suffrage Movement in Washington." *Pacific Northwest Quarterly* 67, no. 2 (April 1976): 49–62.

"The Million Dollar Corner: The Development of Downtown Spokane, 1890–1920." *Pacific Northwest Quarterly* (April 1971): 77–85.

Morrisey, Katherine G. *Mental Territories: Mapping the Inland Empire.* Ithaca, NY: Cornell University Press, 1997.

Moynahan, Jay. *Red Light Revelations: Unveiling Spokane's Risqué Past, 1885–1905.* Spokane, WA: Chickadee Publishing, 1999.

———. *Spokane's Sportin' Women.* Spokane, WA: Chickadee Publishing, 2001.

Moynihan, Ruth Barnes. "Of Women's Rights and Freedom." In *Women in Pacific Northwest History*, ed. Karen Blair. Seattle: University of Washington Press, 2001.

———. *Rebel for Rights: Abigail Scott Duniway.* New Haven, CT: Yale University Press, 1983.

Muncy, Robyn. *Creating a Female Dominion in American Reform, 1890–1935.* New York: Oxford University Press, 1991.

Murphy, Mary. "The Private Lives of Public Women: Prostitution in Butte, Montana, 1878–1917." In *The Women's West*, eds. Susan Armitage and Elizabeth Jameson. Norman: University of Oklahoma Press, 1987.

Northwest Black Pioneers: A Centennial Tribute. Seattle, WA: Bon Marche, 1989.

Popejoy, Don, and Penny Hutton. *Early Spokane.* Charleston, SC: Arcadia Publishing, 2010.

Powers, Dorothy. "All of Us: Spokane Blacks Helped Build City in Many Ways." *Spokesman-Review*, February 7, 1985.

Pratt, Grace Roffey. "The Great-Hearted Huttons in the Coeur d'Alenes." *Montana* (April 1967): 20–33.

Pratt, Orville. *The Story of Spokane.* Spokane, WA: Self-published, 1935.

Raymer, Charles D. *Raymers' Dictionary of Spokane, A Complete Encyclopaedic Dictionary of Spokane and the Inland Empire.* Spokane, WA: Allied Printing, 1906.

"Requiem for a High Roller." *Spokane Magazine* (October 1979): 34–35, 73–77.

Ross-Nazzal, Jennifer M. *Winning the West for Women: The Life of Suffragist Emma Smith DeVoe.* Seattle: University of Washington Press, 2011.

Schrapps, Marcia O'Neill, SNJM, and Nancy G. Compau. *Our City Spokane.* Spokane, WA: Lawton Printing Company, 1996.

Schwantes, Carlos Arnaldo. *The Pacific Northwest: An Interpretive History.* West Point, CT: Praeger, 1995.

Shideler, John C. *A Century of Caring: The Sisters of Providence at Sacred Heart Medical Center.* Spokane, WA: Ross Printing Company, 1986.

Six, Eva Gayle. *Jennie's Tiger: A Woman's Pioneering Stand in an Untamed Corner of Washington State.* N.p.: Xlibris Corporation, 2011.
The Spokane Spokesman Annual Illustrated Supplement. Spokane, WA: 1892.
Stevenson, Shanna. *Women's Votes, Women's Voices: The Campaign for Equal Rights in Washington.* Tacoma: Washington State Historical Society, 2009.
Stillman, Edith Cowley. "Recollections of Henry T. and Lucy A. Peet Cowley." In *The First Fifty Years, Westminster (First) Congregation Church, 1879–1929*, ed. Mary Knox Pope, et al. Spokane, WA: Empire Printing Company, 1929.
Stratton, David H. *Spokane and the Inland Empire: An Interior Pacific Northwest Anthology.* Pullman: Washington State University Press, 2005.
Trunk, Carl H. *History of the City of Spokane, from 1880 to the Lilac Parades.* Spokane, WA: M. Kienholz, 1968.
"When the Dutch Owned Spokane." *Pacific Northwest Quarterly* 72, no. 1 (January 1981): 2–10.

INDEX

ABOUT THE AUTHOR

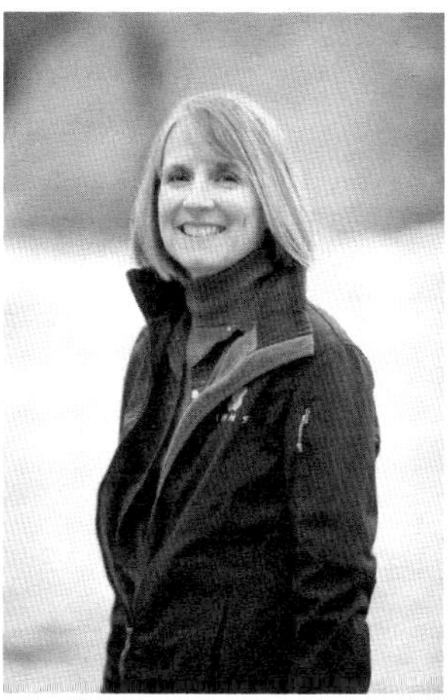

NANCY DRISCOL ENGLE lives and writes from her adopted hometown of Spokane, Washington. She was one of the scholars interviewed for *Courage in Corsets*, a video produced by KSPS television, studying the movement that culminated in giving women the right to vote in Washington in 1910. She won a grant that collaborated with Eastern Washington University, the Museum of Arts and Culture and the Spokane chapter of League of Women Voters to produce a study of the local campaign for the Equal Rights Amendment, for the Washington Women's History Consortium. The results of the study are available online at washingtonhistory.org. She also collaborated with a National Endowment for the Humanities grant with TINCAN, Spokane. She published "We Don't Intend to Take Advice from Women" for *Columbia Magazine*, a study of the police matron controversy in Spokane.